BIOETHICS

Bioethics: 50 Puzzles, Problems, and Thought Experiments collects 50 cases—both real and imaginary—that have been, or should be, of special interest and importance to philosophical bioethics. Cases are collected together under topical headings in a natural order for an introductory course in bioethics. Each case is described in a few pages, which includes bioethical context, a concise narrative of the case itself, and a discussion of its importance, both for broader philosophical issues and for practical problems in clinical ethics and health policy. Each entry also contains a brief, annotated, list of suggested readings. In addition to the classic cases in bioethics, the book contains discussion of cases that involve several emerging bioethical issues: especially, issues around disability, social justice, and the practice of medicine in a diverse and globalized world.

Key Features:

- Gives readers all chapters presented in an identical format:
  - The Case
  - Responses
  - Suggested Readings
- Includes reference to up-to-date literature in journals devoted both to more generalist ethics and to bioethics
- Offers short and self-contained chapters, allowing students to quickly understand an issue and giving instructors flexibility in assigning readings to match the themes of the course
- Features actual or lightly fictionalized cases in humanitarian aid, offering a type of case that is often underrepresented in bioethics books

- Authored by three scholars who are actively involved in the central research areas of bioethics

Sean D. Aas is a Senior Research Scholar at the Kennedy Institute of Ethics and Assistant Professor in the Philosophy Department at Georgetown University. His primary areas of research are bioethics and social and political philosophy, with a significant focus on issues of disability: disability as social construct, disability and political egalitarianism, disability, and health.

Collin O'Neil is an Associate Professor in the Philosophy Department at Lehman College, City University of New York. He teaches and writes on applied ethics, especially medical and clinical research ethics, and topics in legal philosophy.

Chiara Lepora has worked for Médecins Sans Frontières since 2002 and is currently Head of the Manson Unit for MSF UK. She is a medical doctor who conducts research on the ethics of humanitarian assistance and coauthored, with Robert E. Goodin, the book *On Complicity and Compromise* (2013).

PUZZLES, PARADOXES, AND THOUGHT EXPERIMENTS IN PHILOSOPHY

Imaginative cases—or what might be called puzzles, paradoxes, and other thought experiments—play a central role in philosophy. This series offers students and researchers a wide range of such imaginative cases, with each volume devoted fifty such cases in a major subfield of philosophy. Every book in the series includes: some initial background information on each case, a clear and detailed description of the case, and an explanation of the issue(s) to which the case is relevant. Key responses to the case and suggested readings lists are also included.

Recently Published Volumes:

EPISTEMOLOGY
KEVIN MCCAIN

FREE WILL AND HUMAN AGENCY
GARRETT PENDERGRAFT

PHILOSOPHY OF LANGUAGE
MICHAEL P. WOLF

AESTHETICS
MICHEL-ANTOINE XHIGNESSE

PHILOSOPHY OF MIND
TORIN ALTER, AMY KIND, AND ROBERT J. HOWELL

BIOETHICS
SEAN AAS, COLLIN O'NEIL, AND CHIARA LEPORA

Forthcoming Volumes:

ETHICS
SARAH STROUD AND DANIEL MUÑOZ

METAPHYSICS
SAM COWLING, WESLEY D. CRAY, AND KELLY TROGDON

BIOETHICS

50 PUZZLES, PROBLEMS, AND THOUGHT EXPERIMENTS

Sean D. Aas, Collin O'Neil, and Chiara Lepora

NEW YORK AND LONDON

Designed cover image: manuelakanolo via Pixabay

First published 2024
by Routledge
605 Third Avenue, New York, NY 10158

and by Routledge
4 Park Square, Milton Park, Abingdon, Oxon, OX14 4RN

Routledge is an imprint of the Taylor & Francis Group, an informa business

Library of Congress Cataloging-in-Publication Data
A catalog record for this title has been requested

ISBN: 978-1-032-63812-6 (hbk)
ISBN: 978-1-032-63811-9 (pbk)
ISBN: 978-1-032-64052-5 (ebk)

DOI: 10.4324/9781032640525

Typeset in Bembo
by codeMantra

a fetus has a right to life, but also, whether that right is violated when the mother exercises her right to decide what happens to her body.

We generally discuss our puzzles and problem cases the way they are discussed in the professional bioethics literature—which is, we should note, not always the way they are discussed in the bioethics classroom. One thing that often happens in a bioethics class, which this book generally doesn't do, is to lay out and apply broader moral theories, like utilitarianism, virtue theory, or deontology, to concrete issues. Our hope is to give a feel for how working bioethicists engage these issues; our sense is that, though it is possible and sometimes very useful to analyze cases in terms of general philosophical theories, this is not how the bioethical discussion around most of our cases has proceeded. (There are some exceptions, including the case we discuss in Chapter 1, which is centrally about morality in general!) Readers interested in going deeper on the intersection of moral theory and bioethics can supplement their thinking using one of the many fine general bioethics textbooks available, or by taking a course where an instructor puts the cases presented here in contact with primary sources on the main philosophical theories of morality.

That said, it is worth asking, at the outset, why we should be confident that there is anything intellectually worthwhile, in the sort of case-first approach this book exemplifies. That brings us to broader issues in philosophical methodology. How should we understand the evidence that reflection on particular cases—real or imaginary—gives us? If we think of our "intuitions" about cases just as feelings of approval or disapproval, it is not clear why they would help us get at the moral truth. But if we think of intuition as more like perception, it is not clear why it should be trusted. We can tell a story about why our senses are reliable, a story that involves understanding how our eyes and ears and brains work and how they help our beliefs track what is actually happening in the world. This seems impossible for intuitions. Moreover, there is reason to worry that ethical intuition is actually *unreliable*, not just that we do not know that it is reliable. People disagree radically on ethical matters, apparently in good faith. The moral truth, if it is out there, does not seem to stand ready to settle disagreements the way the empirical truth does.

None of these critiques, however, is decisive in itself. People were probably justified in believing their senses even before they knew why their senses were reliable. Even the evident fact of massive moral disagreement is hardly decisive here. People disagree about obvious things like the shape of the Earth or the efficacy of vaccines—that does not mean that our perceptions about these matters are unreliable or must be discarded. And intuitions or something like them seem hard to do entirely without, in philosophy generally or ethics specifically. What would an argument against all moral intuitions be based on, ultimately, except the judgment that some principle of evidence inconsistent with it is simply too intuitive, too important to understanding how we should think across a range of cases, to be given up?

We don't need to settle these difficult questions here, in this book on bioethics, though we hope that considering your intuitions about the cases in the book provides a good impetus to reflection on these methodological matters as well. To find a book like this useful, it is enough to think that each of us can improve our own thinking about bioethical matters by trying to achieve consistency between our principle and our judgments about particular cases. Faced with a case, you need not ask yourself: is my reaction to this a reflection of ultimate moral reality? You need only ask: what *is* my intuitive reaction, about the question the case is meant to pose? What *am I* inclined to say, here, and is saying it consistent with what I want to say about morality more generally, or in other concrete cases? If not, you can use the case to improve your ethical outlook in one of two ways: you can either change your view about the puzzle, problem case, or thought experiment, in light of your more general principles; or you can adjust your confidence in those principles themselves, changing what predilections and presuppositions you bring to future ethical dilemmas. By this process you can reach what philosophers call "reflective equilibrium"; a coherent and thoughtful set of moral principles and reactions. If this is something you're interested in—read on!

Before that, a note of acknowledgment: thanks to Andy Beck at Routledge for conceiving this series and proposing this volume to us. Thanks, as well, to Donald Campbell, Marcello Di Bello, Martine Flokstra, Sean Healy, Betsy Kim, D. Robert MacDougall, Marsha O'Neil, Robert Onus, Andrew Peterson, and David Wasserman for useful discussion or comments on drafts

PART I

BIOETHICS AND PHILOSOPHICAL METHODOLOGY

These cases are contrasted in much more detail in:

Thomson, Judith Jarvis. 1976. "Killing, Letting Die, and the Trolley Problem." *The Monist* 59 (2): 204–17.

For discussion of utilitarian responses, on the transplant in particular, see:

MacAskill, W., D. Meissner, and R.Y. Chappell. 2022. "The Rights Objection." In R.Y. Chappell, D. Meissner, and W. MacAskill (eds.), *An Introduction to Utilitarianism.* https://www.utilitarianism.net/objections-to-utilitarianism/rights, accessed 1/18/2023.

Defending the relevance of intention in cases like this:

Quinn, Warren S. 1989. "Actions, Intentions, and Consequences: The Doctrine of Double Effect." *Philosophy & Public Affairs* 18 (4): 334–51. https://www.jstor.org/stable/2265475

Thomson's own later reconsideration, in favor of a more robustly deontological view, can be found in:

Thomson, Judith Jarvis. 2008. "Turning the Trolley." *Philosophy & Public Affairs* 36 (4): 359–74. http://www.jstor.org/stable/40212830.

For a detailed—indeed, intricately detailed—recent discussion, including a response to Thomson's early and late views on the matter, see:

Kamm, Frances. 2013. "Who Turned the Trolley?" Tanner Lecture on Human Values, University of California, Berkeley. https://tannerlectures.utah.edu/_resources/documents/a-to-z/k/Kamm%20Lecture.pdf

2

BIOETHICS AS METAPHYSICS
The Brain Transplant

THE CASE

What sorts of thing are we, who are writing this book, and reading it? Many will be inclined to answer: we are animals, if maybe special ones: bipedal, rational primates, members of the species *homo sapiens*. To some this view of what we are will seem central to a modern, scientific worldview, to seeing us as part of the natural world rather than standing over or outside it (Olson 1999). Yet, it is surprisingly easy to put pressure on this thought. Philosophers going back at least to John Locke (1689) have imagined the possibility of "switching bodies"—waking up one day in someone else's feet, as well as their shoes. Early examples of this (like Locke's) seem to conflict with what we know about the relation between minds and brains, supposing that your persona can be separated from the neural connections that actually store and manifest it.

More recently philosophers (Shoemaker 1963) have proposed a version that seems more scientifically plausible:

> After a long battle with (non-brain) cancer, your body is shutting down, riddled with tumors. A surgeon comes to you with a startling proposal: he is certain he can take your brain out of your body and place it in the empty skull of a recently deceased cadaver, donated expressly for the purpose.

DOI: 10.4324/9781032640525-3

Your old body will be kept alive, using life support, for research purposes. Do you agree to the deal?

Now, in the real world, a surgeon offering this procedure (and some have) would not be able to promise any real chance of success (and, of course, the offer would raise all sorts of ethical issues; see Wolpe 2017). But the case has us imagine she could. Many of us would be tempted to take the deal in that case: this, we might think, is our only chance of survival.

But: if you are an animal, this case seems actually to offer you no chance of survival at all. For, your brain is just one of the organs of your organic body. You can't move an animal by moving just one of its organs. If you are an animal, then you don't go anywhere when your brain is transplanted. You just become brainless (while the donated body your brain goes to gets a new brain, and with it, presumably, a personality a lot like yours …). Many of us, however, will think that we do have reason to take the deal—that if the surgery works, we will be gaining a body rather than losing a brain. After all, somebody will be walking around with our memories, our plans, our personality— and who would that be, if not us? But if that's true, if we go with the brain, and not the body, then it looks like we can't be animals, since it seems intuitive to say the animal that I was stays right where it is, on the "donor" bed, all throughout this procedure.

RESPONSES

What might we be, if not human animals? Some philosophers think that examples like this show that we are parts of animals—specifically, brains: you go with your brain, so your brain must be you (McMahan 2002). This view, though, can seem to put too much weight on the particular "hardware" that realizes the "software" of your mind: why is my particular brain so important, if what we really care about is the psychology that makes me?

Others think that we can imagine cases where your mind and memories are transferred or "uploaded" into a new body even though your brain itself isn't—those philosophers think we are something more like a *mind* (Chalmers 2010). These "software" version of the mind view face problems of their own, however. If you are just a bunch of thoughts and memories, what happens if those are copied, so that there are two bodies walking around saying and thinking the kinds of things you think and say? These people would be similar, but not one and the same; so, you can't be identical to both of them at once. But which one are you? The mind view seems to offer no way to say (and in some cases, as when there is a clear "copy" and "original," animalism does). And for many people it is hard to shake the force of the claim that we, you, and I are animals, if special ones.

Still, animalists have to explain what is going on in the brain trans-plant. They can do this in two ways. They can try to convince us that the animal actually goes with the brain, or they can argue that you, the human being, actually stays with the brainless body, despite what many are inclined to say when they first hear of the example.

One argument that the animal actually goes with the brain points out that the brain is not just an organ like any other. What makes an animal an animal, so the argument goes, is that its parts are working together in a certain way, that they are integrated by functions like immunity, metabolism, and circulation. But many if not most of these unifying functions are managed by the brain, in higher animals like us. This is why, for instance, many people think that humans *die* or *cease to exist* when and only when their brain ceases to exist (see Chapter 27 for discussion). If this is the case, then you go with your brain even if you are an animal (Van Inwagen 1990).

This response, however, has limited force against a modified version of the case. For it turns out that the parts of the brain that realize your memories, thoughts, and personality—the *cerebrum* or *forebrain*—are largely physically separate from the parts (the *hindbrain* or *brain-stem*) that manage the body's physiological functions. So, we can just imagine that what is transplanted is the thought-making parts, the higher-brain, not the physiology-managing part. In that case, it looks like the animal really would stay in the bed, albeit in a persistent veg-etative state. But it still seems to many of us that you would go with your cerebrum, waking up in your new body.

Most people who think we are animals will think that you defi-nitely stay with your body and lower brain in the cerebrum transplant case. They will say this despite the fact that the new body, with what has always so far been your cerebrum, will be the only body around saying that it is you, trying to do the sorts of things you were trying to do, and so on. Animalists, generally, will admit that this claim of theirs is counterintuitive. But they will argue that we shouldn't always base our views on far-out science-fiction cases. Rather, sometimes, we have to (as philosophers say) "bite bullets," say things that seem initially wrong, about a thought experiment. We have to do this, they will say, when there is no good alternative. And they will think that this is the case here: that it is so hard to make sense of the idea that we are mind, or brains, instead of full-on animals, that we should change our interpretation of the experiment to fit our theory, rather than changing the theory to accommodate the experiment.

Animalists probably have at least part of the truth here on how we should think of these issues. That is, we won't settle hard philosophical questions about what we are just by considering one hypothetical case. Still, cases like these at least help illustrate concrete implications of otherwise-abstract metaphysical theories of what we are, helping us to understand what these different theories really mean. And, even if not decisive, they do seem to provide some sort of evidence, in this case a prima facie argument that animalists must address.

SUGGESTED READINGS

The brain transplant case was first raised by Sydney Shoemaker, in the context of personal identity, in:
> Shoemaker, Sydney. 1963. *Self-Knowledge and Self-Identity*. Contemporary Philosophy. Ithaca, NY: Cornell University Press.

The most famous defense of the view that we are not animals at all, but rather "persons," goes all the way back to:
> Locke, J. (1689) *An Essay Concerning Human Understanding* (The Clarendon Edition of the Works of John Locke), ed. Peter H. Nidditch, Oxford: Oxford University Press, 1975. doi:10.1093/actrade/9780198243861.book.1

For a sophisticated defense of the view that we humans are essentially "embodied mind," not whole animals but only the thinking parts thereof, see:
> McMahan, Jeff. 2002. *The Ethics of Killing: Problems at the Margins of Life*. New York: Oxford University Press.

For discussion of the alternative view, on which we are more like the software that "runs on" the brain than the hardware (wetware) it runs on:
> Chalmers, David J. 2010. "The Singularity: A Philosophical Analysis." *Journal of Consciousness Studies* 17 (9–10). https://consc.net/papers/singularity.pdf.

For an extended defense of the claim that you "go with your brain" even if you are an animal, see:

van Inwagen, Peter. 1990. *Material Beings*. Ithaca, NY: Cornell University Press.

For a book-length, defense of the view that we are (entire) animals, see:

Olson, Eric T. 1999. *The Human Animal*. Oxford: Oxford University Press. https://doi.org/10.1093/0195134230.001.0001.

Finally, for discussion of real-world attempts at head transplants, and their (highly dubious!) ethics:

Wolpe, Paul Root. 2017. "Ahead of Our Time: Why Head Transplantation Is Ethically Unsupportable." *AJOB Neuroscience* 8 (4): 206–10. https://doi.org/10.1080/21507740.2017.1392386.

3

BIOETHICS ACROSS CULTURES

The Farewell

THE CASE

A central principle of ethical medical care is *informed consent*: that physicians cannot ethically treat patients unless those patients know why they are being treated, what risks and benefits treatment might have, and agree to the treatment in light of those risks and benefits. But this norm, like many norms, is understood differently in different cultural contexts.

The 2019 film *The Farewell*, written and directed by Lulu Wang, presents a vivid narrative that illustrates a different perspective on whether and when patients should be informed about what is going on with their health. In *The Farewell*—which is fictional, but based on a true story—a Chinese-American woman, Billi, struggles with her family's decision not to tell her grandmother, Nai Nai, that she has been diagnosed with terminal cancer. Initially deeply disturbed by this apparent denial of autonomy, and tempted to tell Nai Nai herself, Billi comes over the course of the film to have a more nuanced view. She sees, among other things, that her family believes that Nai Nai has nothing to gain from knowing, since she will follow the doctor's recommendation no matter what the rationale for it. And she comes to see that knowing might even be harmful to her grandmother. Most

DOI: 10.4324/9781032640525-4

of all, she comes to appreciate the difficulty of these issues, and the knotty problem of who should get to decide who knows what.

RESPONSES

The Farewell and the many real-world cases like it raise several important ethical issues. The most basic is the simple question, whether the family's actions in withholding information are permissible or not. Billi's family thinks that it is, for three main reasons (Wang 2019).

The first is that, as one character puts it, "it is not the cancer that kills you, it is the fear." The idea is that there is something like a negative placebo or "nocebo" effect here, where stress about imminent death actually damages the body, making death come more quickly (see Hancock et al. 2007, and Chapter 22 below, for discussion). The story is consistent with the empirical premise of this argument. That said, there appears as yet to be no reliable evidence about this, given the obvious ethical difficulties of conducting a trial comparing people with knowledge of their diagnosis and people from that knowledge is withheld. There are also reasons to doubt that withholding information is beneficial. Deceit itself can be psychologically, and thus possibly physically, harmful, if it is discovered or even suspected. Moreover, even if it were better for the patient not to know, that would hardly resolve the issue—people may sometime be entitled to information that would harm them, or which they might regret knowing after hearing it. But it is hard to see how to respect this entitlement, if patients do not know they have it.

A second argument for withholding information about terminal diagnoses relates to this last point. In the film, it's revealed that Nai Nai herself participated in a similar deception involving her own husband, who died of cancer years earlier. This may be evidence that she herself would prefer not to know in the same situation. That said, this past behavior is far short of an explicit request not to be told about any terminal diagnosis she herself would receive. We do not, after all, always treat others as we would like to be treated. And even if Nai Nai had made an explicit request here, it would not be entirely clear that this prior wish expresses her current perspective—sometimes, when actually faced with a big decision like this, we change our minds. She will never have this opportunity, if she is not told (though, conversely, if she is told and finds she still wishes she had not been, this cannot be reversed either).

A final argument goes to deeper philosophical issues about ethics across cultures. Says a member of Billi's family: "You think one's life belongs to one's self. But that's the difference between the East and the West—in the East a person's life is part a whole: family, society." This character denies that the value of *autonomy*, individual self-determination, has the same significance in China as in the United States (in this context, see Wang et al. 2018). Rather, because of cultural differences, the family ought to have substantially more say (Chen and Fan 2010). If we take this as a moral point rather than an observation about prevailing practices, it implies a position philosophers call *cultural relativism*.

Relativism itself can be understood in various ways, as this case illustrates (Gowans 2021). The most robust version says that ultimate ethical standards depend on culture, such that, at the end of the day, the only explanation for why informed consent is ethically required in the US but not in China is that people in China have different beliefs and desires about these matters. This can seem like the tolerant, enlightened view here. But if all that it takes to make a practice permissible is that people believe it is, then there are no limits to what a culture could, in principle, construct as a just practice. Apparently awful practices like slavery or female genital mutilation would be acceptable so long as they are approved of by the culture in which they occur.

More moderate forms of "relativism" may be more plausible. On this kind of view, facts about cultural values and preferences shape, without fully determining, what is morally permissible. So, for instance, we might think that there is a trans-cultural requirement that we give people the information they can be expected to want about their health condition. In the West, we expect that most people would want to know if they are terminally ill, so much so that in practice it will rarely be appropriate to withhold this information. In China, and maybe other places besides, there is reason to believe that many patients, patients like Nai Nai, would not want this information (perhaps because they believe that their family can and should make good decisions, without telling them) (Sarafis 2014). In that situation, a trans-cultural principle has different implications, because it makes what we should do dependent on facts that vary across cultural contexts.

SUGGESTED READINGS

For the film itself, see:

Wang, Lulu. 2019. *The Farewell*. United States: A24.

One ethically sophisticated review can be found in:

Lu, Donna. 2019. "The Farewell Explores the Ethics of Lying about a Cancer Diagnosis." *New Scientist*, October 2019. https://www.newscientist.com/article/2221673-the-farewell-explores-the-ethics-of-lying-about-a-cancer-diagnosis/.

On the ethics of family input in a Chinese Confucian context (defending a substantial role for the family in consent processes):

Chen, X., and R. Fan (2010). "The Family and Harmonious Medical Decision Making: Cherishing an Appropriate Confucian Moral Balance." *The Journal of Medicine and Philosophy* 35 (5): 573–86. https://doi.org/10.1093/jmp/jhq046

For an empirical study of Chinese physician's attitudes towards the sharing of diagnoses, finding much reluctance to disclose to patients without the family's agreement, see:

Wang, Hongchun, Fang Zhao, Xiangling Wang, and Xiaoyang Chen. 2018. "To Tell or Not: The Chinese Doctors' Dilemma on Disclosure of a Cancer Diagnosis to the Patient." *Iranian Journal of Public Health* 47 (11): 1773–4. https://pubmed.ncbi.nlm.nih.gov/30581799.

Useful surveys of more general empirical issues around disclosure include:

Hancock, Karen, Josephine M. Clayton, Sharon M. Parker, Sharon Walder, Phyllis N. Butow, Sue Carrick, David Currow, et al. 2007. "Truth-Telling in Discussing Prognosis in Advanced Life-Limiting Illnesses: A Systematic Review." *Palliative Medicine* 21 (6): 507–17. https://doi.org/10.1177/0269216307080823.

Sarafis, Pavlos, Andreas Tsounis, Maria Malliarou, and Eleni Lahana. 2014. "Disclosing the Truth: A Dilemma between Instilling Hope and Respecting Patient Autonomy in Everyday Clinical Practice." *Global Journal of Health Science* 6 (2): 128–37. https://doi.org/10.5539/gjhs.v6n2p128.

On moral relativism, and its problems, more generally, one good place to start is:

Gowans, Chris. 2021. "Moral Relativism." In *The Stanford Encyclopedia of Philosophy*, edited by Edward N Zalta, Spring 2021. Metaphysics Research Lab, Stanford University. https://plato.stanford.edu/archives/spr2021/entries/moral-relativism/

PART II

CREATING LIFE

4

SHOULD I HAVE CHILDREN?
The Islanders and the Cube

THE CASE

No one passes through life entirely unscathed. Even the best lives contain pain, suffering, illnesses, disappointments, and ultimately death. Since we could not ask to be born, we never consented to suffer these harms. Does this mean that our parents have wronged us in creating us? Do they owe us compensation for the inevitable burdens that come with life, even if our burdens are no greater than most people's?

Ethicists often defend procreation with an analogy, the "Rescue Case." Driver is knocked unconscious in a traffic accident and Rescuer sees that Driver is in danger of dying unless he can be removed from the car quickly. Rescuer also sees that the only way to remove Driver will require breaking his arm. If Rescuer does break Driver's arm without his consent in the process of saving his life, intuitively, Rescuer owes him no apology, and it would be absurd for Driver to demand that Rescuer pay the medical costs of repairing the break. Similarly, parents might argue, although they knew our lives would contain harms, they also believed it highly likely that the benefits would more than compensate for those harms, so that we would be better off on balance.

Seana Shiffrin finds this defense of procreation unconvincing (Shiffrin 1999). She concedes that Driver has no grounds for complaint

DOI: 10.4324/9781032640525-6

about or compensation for the broken arm but claims that the following "Gold Cube case" is a closer analogy to procreation.

In this case, Wealthy is searching for a meaningful project and decides to bestow some of his vast wealth on the people living on the neighboring island. They are living quite comfortably but they could still spend additional money in ways that would make them significantly better off. One problem is that the neighboring island has no paper currency and due to political tensions Wealthy is neither permitted to travel there nor to communicate with the inhabitants. Wealthy's solution is to craft 100 cubes of gold each worth 5 million dollars and to fly over the island and drop the cubes near people so that they will spot them and retrieve them. He does his best to avoid hitting anyone but cannot eliminate the risk entirely and one person, Unlucky, does get hit by a cube, which breaks his arm. But he also retrieves the cube and is 5 million dollars richer, so that Wealthy's dropping of the cube still leaves Unlucky better off overall.

According to Shiffrin, even though Unlucky is, despite his broken arm, much better off on balance, Wealthy owes Unlucky an apology and special compensation for his broken arm. If we agree, Shiffrin claims that we ought to draw a similar conclusion about procreation: no matter how well our lives go, our parents owe us an apology for having imposed life on us and special support in managing the harms that inevitably come with it. One advantage of Shiffrin's position is that it explains something that would otherwise be puzzling; namely, why we expect parents, who have already bestowed the gift of life on their children, to bestow additional aid when needed even when their children's lives would have remained well worth living without it (Cholbi 2017). But is Shiffrin's argument persuasive?

RESPONSES

According to Shiffrin, although Driver and Unlucky are each made better off on balance, there is a crucial difference—Driver will suffer a harm if Rescuer does not act, while Unlucky will not.

Shiffrin argues that what it is for someone to suffer a harm is simply to be in a state that is bad for that person, regardless of whether this state is worse in some respect for the person compared with some alternative state they had been in or would otherwise have been in. Broken arms, pain, injuries, disabilities, losses, the destruction of valued relationships and projects, and death are bad for a person. Similarly, a pure benefit—that is, a benefit that is not merely the absence or prevention of harm—is a state that is positively good for a person, regardless of whether this state is better than some alternative state. Having 20/10 vision, enjoying fine food, developing one's talent for the piano, and more generally the fulfillment of desires whose nonfulfillment would not be harmful are examples of pure benefits.

Applying this account of harms and benefits, we can say that Rescuer caused a lesser harm to Driver (broken arm) to prevent Driver from suffering a much greater harm (loss of life). We cannot say that Wealthy caused a lesser harm to Unlucky (broken arm) to prevent him from suffering some greater harm. Recall that the islanders were living comfortably and do not need the windfall to alleviate any badness in their lives. Rather, Wealthy harmed Unlucky to give him access to pure benefits, e.g., travelling, pursuing a master's degree in art history, acquiring a boat, and dining at nice restaurants.

Here is the lesson we are meant to draw from Rescue and Gold Cube. What Rescue shows is that when getting consent is not possible, we do not wrong someone by causing them to suffer a lesser harm when this is necessary to prevent them from suffering a greater harm. What Gold Cube shows is that when getting consent is not possible, we can wrong someone by causing them to suffer a lesser harm to bestow pure benefits on them, even when those benefits more than compensate for the harm.

If this lesson is correct, the implication for procreation is clear. Procreation inevitably results in harms. Normally existence also bestows access to benefits that leaves the person better off overall. But it does not make them better off by preventing or alleviating greater harms or any harms at all. No harm can be suffered by a merely possible person, and so there is no harm to be alleviated or prevented by making a possible person actual. Thus, procreation imposes harms on the person brought into existence just for the sake of bestowing pure benefits on them, and it obviously does so without obtaining that person's consent. Insofar as Gold Cube is an apt analogy for procreation, we should conclude that we were all wronged by our parents and are owed compensation.

Many ethicists are inclined to resist Shiffrin's argument. One way to resist it, while still conceding there is a moral difference between Rescue and Gold Cube, is to come up with a better explanation for that moral difference than that the first involves harm prevention and the second benefit bestowal (Boonin 2014). Another way is to argue that Gold Cube is not an apt analogy for procreation. Shiffrin anticipates one objection in this vein. Before the cube is dropped, Unlucky exists and has autonomy rights. Because he did not waive those rights via consent, he is wronged by Wealthy's dropping of the cube. But there is no individual who exists prior to procreation that could be wronged by having life imposed on them without their consent. Shiffrin concedes that, unlike Wealthy's cube dropping, procreation does not infringe anyone's rights until later when there is an actual person who suffers harm. But the fact that procreation will eventually lead to the infringement of an actual person's rights can still give us a duty to avoid it now, just as we have a duty not to plant a time bomb set to go off in seven years in the basement of a kindergarten, even though none of the future victims exists now (Shiffrin 1999; also see Weinberg 2015 who develops a version of this objection).

Some philosophers have also challenged the analogy between Gold Cube and procreation by arguing that there is an important difference in the way the harms come about in the two cases. In the case of Unlucky, dropping the cube directly causes harm and does so in a way that infringes one of Unlucky's rights—specifically his right to bodily integrity. Procreation, by contrast, merely puts someone in a situation where they will inevitably be directly harmed by natural forces and other people. Ethicists have marked this difference by saying that dropping the gold cube *imposes* harms while procreation merely *exposes* someone to harms (Degrazia 2014). One way to test the significance of this distinction would be to revise the Gold Cube case so that it was only Unlucky's *possession* of the gold cube that attracted certain harms. Perhaps Wealthy could foresee that there was a high probability that Unlucky's windfall would prompt a bully to break his arm out of envy or would strain one of Unlucky's friendships beyond the breaking point. If in the revised case it seems much less obvious that Unlucky was wronged by Wealthy's cube dropping, despite still being on balance better off, then we should hesitate to transfer our conclusions about the original Gold Cube to procreation.

SUGGESTING READINGS

An important article, not just for the anti-natalist line of reasoning, but also for its influential objections to comparative accounts of harms and its alternative non-comparative account:

Seana Shiffrin, 1999. "Wrongful Life, Procreative Responsibility, and the Significance of Harm." *Legal Theory* 5: 117–48.

Recruits Shiffrin's argument that procreation wrongs the child to justify parental obligations:

Cholbi, Michael. 2017. "How Procreation Generates Parental Rights and Obligations." In Michael Cholbi and Jaime Ahlberg (eds.), *Procreation, Parenthood, and Educational Rights: Ethical and Philosophical Issues* (pp. 15–36). New York: Routledge.

For a debate between a prominent anti-natalist and opponent of anti-natalism, which also contains criticism of Shiffrin's argument:

Benatar, David, and David Wasserman. 2015. *Debating Procreation: Is It Wrong to Reproduce?* Oxford: Oxford University Press.

For an engagingly written book that presents a qualified defense of procreation against arguments like Shiffrin's:

Weinberg, Rivka. 2015. *The Risk of a Lifetime: How, When, and Why Procreation May Be Permissible*. New York: Oxford University Press.

A good source of objection to Shiffrin's argument:

Boonin, David, 2014. *The Non-Identity Problem and the Ethics of Future People*. New York: Oxford University Press.

For the argument that Shiffrin's analogy to procreation fails because procreation exposes the child to harms while Wealthy imposes harms on Unlucky:

DeGrazia, David. 2014. "Chapter 5: Bearing Children in Wrongful Life Cases." In *Creation Ethics* (pp. 137–62). Oxford: Oxford University Press.

5

WHICH CHILDREN SHOULD I HAVE, I?
The Non-Identity Problem

THE CASE

Parenting is one of the most morally important things that people do. Much of this importance lies in the profound significance of the care parents provide for their children as they grow up. But creating a person is a major decision in its own right. It matters what kind of lives people live, and which children parents have makes a difference to which people get to live which sorts of lives. A famous pair of cases, adapted (by David Boonin, 2008) from an example of Derek Parfit's (1984), illustrates the distinction:

Betty: Betty is currently pregnant. Her doctor tells her that, unless she takes a drug for two months, her child will be born with a significant, but not life-ruining, disease or disability. If she takes it, the child will likely be healthy. Even though the drug has no serious side effects for her or her fetus, Betty chooses not to take the drug, and the child is born with the disease or disability.

Wilma: Wilma is thinking of having a child soon but is not currently pregnant. Her doctor tells her that, if she conceives now, her child will be born with a significant, but not life-ruining, disease or disability. On the other hand, if she takes (a different, just-as-safe) drug for two months, and only conceives afterwards, she is likely to

DOI: 10.4324/9781032640525-7

have a healthy child. She chooses not to take the drug, and a child is born with a disease or disability.

Boonin invites us to conclude that Betty has done something wrong here. But what Wilma does seems similar; and, thus, perhaps, similarly wrong. Yet, as Parfit points out, there is a major difference between cases like Betty's and cases like Wilma's. Betty's choices make someone in particular worse off than they would have been: specifically, her fetus, who (we can assume for now) would be better off healthy than not. But Wilma's child—Boonin calls him "Pebbles"—would not have been born at all if Wilma had acted on her doctor's orders. If she had conceived at a different time, the child would have come from different gametes—a different sperm, and a different ova. Most philosophers agree, then, that Pebbles could not have existed, but for Wilma's (apparently) irresponsible choice. Whatever else Wilma did, then, she did not *harm* anyone, at least in the sense of "harm" on which we harm people only when we make them worse off than they otherwise would have been. More generally, it seems like nobody has a complaint about Wilma's choice—not Pebbles, because he is not harmed, and not the healthier child Wilma might have had instead, since she does not exist to complain.

RESPONSES

This is a version of what philosophers call the *non-identity problem*—the problem of understanding how we should evaluate actions which determine *who* will exist, and not just what will happen to those who already exist. This is a problem especially for those who think that morality is centrally about harms and claims, such that if no one is harmed or wronged by an action, that action is not morally wrong. Philosophers and bioethicists have devised several lines of response meant to save the intuition that having a less happy child, when you could have a more happy one, can be morally wrong.

A first approach is to say that actions like Wilma's are harmful to her child after all, just because they cause suffering and disability. This requires saying how someone can harm a person, with their actions, without making them worse off than they otherwise would have been. Some philosophers think that we can identify harms without making these sorts of *comparisons* to how the harmed person's life would go if things went differently. Rather, we harm someone if our actions ensure that that certain bad things ("non-comparative" harms) happen to them—whether or not these things are *worse* than what would have happened, if we hadn't acted (Shiffrin 1999).

A second, similar approach is to maintain that Wilma's child is wronged but not made worse off (see Chapters 7 and 19 for more on cases like this). The challenge here is to say which right or claim of her child is violated. If the supposed right is an inalienable right against non-comparative harm, it faces the challenges just considered. More plausible (in this case and the limb case) would be to say that we have rights against being put in certain bad states without our *consent*, even if we are not thereby made worse off than we otherwise would have been. However, as Parfit himself points out, this seems to be just the sort of case where *hypothetical* or *implied* consent serves just as well as actual consent; just as an unconscious patient requiring surgery is assumed to consent to harms that make them better off on balance, so too, we might think, can we assume that children like Wilma's would consent to harms in order to get the goods of a life worth living.

A different approach altogether is to give up on the idea that morality is only about the interests and claims of particular, existing people. For instance, we might think that parents like Wilma simply have an obligation to make the world a better place, and that a world with less suffering and disability is a better place than one with more (Savulescu 2001). This proposal, however, faces several problems of its own. For one, it carries the implication that adding disabled people, like Wilma's child, to the world, makes it a worse place; many disabled people would take offense to this, perhaps for good reason (see Chapters 10 and 11). Separately, the idea of doing something wrong, without wronging anybody in particular, seems to be both hard to understand, in this context (who can blame Wilma, for what she did?) and of questionable relevance (if we object to her action, don't we do it on her child's behalf, not on behalf of the state of "the world"?). This last response also applies to attempts to understand the wrong here in terms of imposing costs on people other than Wilma (say, by requiring the health system to provide for her child's care)

Alternatively, we might think that the action is wrong because of what it says about Wilma—that she doesn't have the appropriate level of concern for the well-being of her future family, or for her own interests. She is, among other things, doing a bad job of being a parent (Wasserman 2005). However, if none of the other approaches to understanding what is objectionable about her action works out, it is not clear why Wilma's choice should say anything so bad about her after all: if her action does not harm anyone, or violate anyone's rights, or wrongfully make the world a worse place, then it is not clear why she displays bad character or violates a role-obligation in doing it.

This brings us to a final response. This is to "bite the bullet," accepting that Wilma's action is not morally wrong after all (Boonin 2008). Those sympathetic to the claim that it is not bad to be disabled might be tempted to accept this. But that "mere difference" view is not in itself enough to solve the non-identity problem. Even proponents hold that there are some medical conditions that have a net negative impact on well-being—serious migraines, for instance. If we assume Wilma's child was to develop a condition like this, we would face the original dilemma, whether or not we thought that "merely" disabling condition like blindness or Down Syndrome would raise the problem in the same way. It remains to be seen whether we should embrace the harder-to-swallow conclusion that it is not only foolish but actually morally wrong to bring a child into being who will have a lot of suffering and only a little happiness to compensate, when we can choose to have a different child who will suffer much less instead.

SUGGESTED READINGS

The "non-identity" problem was first discussed in the seminal:
Parfit, Derek. 1984. *Reasons and Persons*. Oxford: Oxford University Press.
For the Betty and Wilma case, and an argument that it is not wrong to bring worse-off people into existence, see:
Boonin, David. 2008. "How to Solve the Non-Identity Problem." *Public Affairs Quarterly* 22 (2): 127–57.
On the idea that choosing the worse-off child can be wrong because it puts them in bad states, whether or not they would have been better states otherwise, see:
Shiffrin, S., 1999. "Wrongful Life, Procreative Responsibility, and the Significance of Harm," *Legal Theory*, 5: 117–48.

On the appropriate attitudes of parents, to their prospective children, see:

Wasserman, David. 2005. "The Nonidentity Problem, Disability, and the Role Morality of Prospective Parents." *Ethics* 116 (1): 132–52. https://doi.org/10.1086/454369.

For the claim that we ought to have the happiest child we can, because that makes the world a better place:

Savulescu, Julian. 2001. "Procreative Beneficence: Why We Should Select the Best Children." *Bioethics* 15 (5): 413–26. https://doi.org/10.1111/1467-8519.00251

6

WHICH CHILDREN SHOULD I HAVE, II?

Gattaca

THE CASE

New reproductive technologies offer us unprecedented control over our future children. Prospective parents can screen for a wide range of diseases and disabilities, as well as non-pathological characteristics like sex. In the future imagined by the 1997 film *Gattaca* (Niccol 1997), parents can choose even more than that—not just avoiding disease, but selecting preferred traits like blue eyes or superior athletic ability. The story of the film concerns two characters: Vincent, stigmatized as an "invalid" for being born "naturally," without intervention, and Jerome, who was genetically enhanced but now suffers from paraplegia and alcoholism after a devastating accident.

Vincent aspires to be an astronaut. However, because he is perceived to be genetically inferior, he can only work at Gattaca, the titular space agency, as a janitor. He and Jerome agree on a conspiracy: Vincent will pay Jerome for biological materials he can use to assume Jerome's identity, thereby qualifying medically for a long-term space mission to Titan. The ruse seems set to succeed, until a murder at Gattaca brings the staff under close scrutiny.

The main action of the film concerns how Vincent and Jerome navigate these events, and the relationship between them as each must

DOI: 10.4324/9781032640525-8

find a way to live in a society that makes a person's genetics their destiny. The movie thus concerns the individual and societal effects of the kind of genetic technologies which were just becoming available in the 1990s, and which have only advanced since. The film's future is not exactly our own future, but it seems clear we will have access to some of the same technologies, and dilemmas, as the characters in *Gattaca* do. This film, therefore, continues to provide an especially fruitful set of thought experiments for considering the ethics of new, emerging, and possible genetic technologies.

RESPONSES

A first set of ethical questions about genetic technologies concern the basic way in which it works (Ogbunugafor et al. 2022). Suppose you want to determine what sort of child you can have, using knowledge of what sequences of DNA cause which traits. You can do so either by *selection*, creating a large number of embryos with random genetic sequences, and choosing to implant and bring to term the one with the traits you want; or by *modification*, taking a single embryo, and changing its DNA so that it will have the traits you want. Both selection and modification are now technologically possible, but only selection is in wide use—primarily for selecting against disease and disability (see Chapter 5 for controversies around this practice), secondarily (and uncommonly) for sex selection, and only occasionally for choosing children with phenotypic traits like athletic ability or eye color.

The distinction between selection and modification may well make a difference to our ethical evaluation of technologies, in at least two ways. The first is that selection itself, like in vitro fertilization, involves the creation of a large number of embryos with the intention of discarding them. If embryos have moral status at all similar to the rest of us, this is likely wrong in itself, since it involves something like killing a number of innocent people (George 2002). The second is about the selected embryo rather than those left behind. Genetic modification changes what would have happened to a single person. This means that parents are responsible for their choice to modify in a particularly direct way: if it goes well, it benefits the child; if it goes poorly, they have harmed the child (as Jerome may have been harmed). In selection, on the other hand, choosing traits is not a matter of changing how a given child will turn out, but rather a matter of choosing which child to have. Assuming modification is not also available, then it will be the case that, however the child turns out, there will be no way for *that* child to have turned out differently. That may make selection, in this way at least, easier to justify than modification.

Another set of question raised by the film relate to the purpose to which genetic technologies are put. Jerome seems to have been modified or selected, not just to avoid genetic disease, but also to have high-level athletic and intellectual abilities. This means that gene technology is used in the film not just to protect health, but in an effort to *enhance* or produce abilities and traits different from those involved in the absence of disease.

Enhancement efforts are controversial in themselves. Some philosophers argue that trying to choose the traits of your child represents the wrong kind of attitude towards them, thinking of them as a means to the end of producing a certain sort of person rather than as valuable in themselves (Sandel 2007). Jerome seems to feel he was wronged in this way—that he was thereby somehow robbed of his ability to be the author of his own life. Vincent, by contrast, seems profoundly self-made, and proud of it. Some philosophers would say he is right to be proud: his accomplishments are more his, and more valuable as accomplishments, because he chose them on his own and was given no "head start" in pursuing them.

Not all philosophers judge the results of genetic enhancement so harshly (Savulescu and Kahane 2009). Parents profoundly influence their children's traits all the time, using low-tech methods like ordinary education. Sometimes these interventions are aimed at giving children certain abilities in the first place (to play the violin, say), sometimes to give them abilities much greater than those of others (to play the violin brilliantly). These efforts—arguably!—need not reflect the wrong kind of attitude towards children as authentic persons. Nor need being educated, or encouraged, or otherwise shaped by our parents' efforts make our accomplishments any less ours, or any less valuable as accomplishment.

Other critiques of enhancement focus more on its social effects than what it means for enhancing parents or enhanced children. The society represented in *Gattaca* seems, not to put too fine a point on it, unjust. This is so even if we abstract from the dark history of the eugenic ("good-genetic") ideas in our own society (the movie itself does not entirely do so; think of the black doctor's mention of "blue eyes" as a desired trait during genetic counseling). The film shows us its world through the eyes of Vincent, a member of a deeply stigmatized class, a class of "invalids" harassed by police and excluded from all but the most menial occupations. The insults and exclusion Vincent experiences are, and are meant to be, revolting, to many of us—*Gattaca* is easy to take as, and maybe meant in part as, a cautionary tale, a dystopian vision of the world that awaits us if genetic technology grows unchecked.

It is, however, important to understand what makes the world of *Gattaca* unjust. Here we can distinguish the essentials of the system in the film from incidental, if predictable, abuses, like insults or brutality directed at "invalids." One argument against genetic modification, to be sure, is that it might be likely to lead to a culture that encourages abuses against the unmodified, including underestimation of their actual abilities. Would the society represented in *Gattaca* still be unjust if the unmodified were treated with dignity and respect? It is not so clear. Consider Vincent himself: if he actually has a strong predisposition to heart disease, perhaps he should not be on a long-term space mission where a problem with his health could endanger the entire crew. There seems to be no unjust "discrimination" in this kind of ordinary medical screening for astronauts. On the other hand, we might be concerned with the inequalities genetic enhancement would produce even, perhaps especially, if those modified to the highest levels of performance are accurately sorted into the most rewarding social positions. In such a system, inequality might be an intended feature, rather than an unintended bug—representing a "meritocracy," in the pejorative sense of a society obsessed with "merit."

That brings us to the relevance of *Gattaca* to our own society. As a work of art some of its meaning is metaphorical, asking us to reflect on how we now understand concepts like ability and achievement in the here and now. But as philosophers we can take it literally too, as a future we might want to promote or avoid. If we think genetic enhancement is wrong as such, then it may be that the development of these kinds of technologies should be discouraged, or even banned (Lander et al. 2019). At the very least, it may make sense to take measures to forbid use of this technology in employment decisions, or more broadly to protect our rights concerning who can access our genetic information and how they can make use of it. If, on the other hand, the injustices represented in *Gattaca* are merely contingent side effects, then it will be worth asking whether there is anything we can do to realize the benefits of genetic technology while mitigating its harms. In this way, philosophical reflection about the film can help to orient our practical thinking: telling us what else we need to know, to know how to feel about different aspects of the future represented in the film.

SUGGESTED READINGS

The film itself:

Niccol, Andrew. 1997. *Gattaca*. United States: Columbia Pictures.

For a recent review of ethical and (especially) scientific issues in the film:

Ogbunugafor, C. Brandon, and Michael D. Edge. 2022. "Gattaca as a Lens on Contemporary Genetics: Marking 25 Years into the Film's 'Not-Too-Distant' Future." *Genetics* 222 (4). https://doi.org/10.1093/genetics/iyac142.

For an argument that implies that, by killing embryos, prenatal genetic selection wrongfully kills beings with full moral status, see:

George, R. 2002. "Statement of Professor George (Joined by Dr. Gómez-Lobo)." In *President's Council on Bioethics: Human Cloning and Human Dignity: An Ethical Inquiry*, 258–66. https://bioethicsarchive.georgetown.edu/pcbe/reports/cloningreport/appendix.html

For broader concerns about enhancement and authenticity, see:

Sandel, Michael J. 2007. *The Case against Perfection: Ethics in the Age of Genetic Engineering*. Cambridge, MA: Belknap Press.

For an influential argument strongly in favor of "procreative beneficence," or having the best child possible, see:

Savulescu, Julian, and Guy Kahane. 2009. "The Moral Obligation to Create Children with the Best Chance of the Best Life." *Bioethics* 23 (5): 274–90. https://doi.org/https://doi.org/10.1111/j.1467-8519.2008.00687.x.

An international group of geneticists recently argued for a moratorium on *some* genetic technologies, here:

Lander, Eric, Feng Zhang, Emmanuelle Charpentier, and Paul Berg. 2019. "Adopt a Moratorium on Heritable Genome Editing." *Nature* 567: 165–86. https://doi.org/10.1038/d41586-019-00726-5.

The term "meritocracy," and the articulation of concerns about it, was coined by Michael Young, in another piece of dystopian fiction:

Young, Michael Dunlop. 1970. *The Rise of the Meritocracy 1870–2033: An Essay on Education and Equality*. Baltimore: Penguin Books.

7

MAKING PEOPLE HAPPY, OR MAKING HAPPY PEOPLE?
The Repugnant Conclusion

THE CASE

Having children is one of the most important decisions a person can make, since it means making new people, and people and their lives have great moral significance. The ethics of procreation is important not just for parents (on which see Chapter 5), but for physicians and public health policy-makers too. Understanding it is especially important for public health policies related to reproductive decision-making, like policies around sex education or contraception. Many people think that policy-makers ought to frame these policies to avoid overpopulation, ensuring that there are enough material and ecological resources so that everyone can live a good life.

Derek Parfit presents us with a set of examples that show that it is not so easy to defend this common-sense view (Parfit 1984). The basic idea is this. If every life is valuable, then a world with more people is better in at least one way: it has more valuable lives in it. This aspect of value can be multiplied the more people we add—so long as those people have lives that are barely worth living. Even if there is also something distinctively valuable about having a world where people are not just barely getting by, the sum of the individual value of each of the much greater number of hard lives we could add will outweigh

DOI: 10.4324/9781032640525-9

it—if there are enough of them. Thus for any small population that is very happy on average, there will always be some larger, perhaps much larger, population that is much less happy on average, but which we should still prefer on the whole, if we take seriously the value of the less-happy lives that could be lived in it.

We can illustrate Parfit's arguments here with a concrete example from the ethics of reproductive technology. Fertility treatments sometimes involve producing many reproductively potent tissues (gametes, like sperm and eggs) which are then discarded (see Chapter 6 for discussion). Suppose it became possible to make viable embryos out of more of these tissues, and cheaply and easily bring them to term (say, in artificial wombs). Suppose also that the biological parents were fine with this (or perhaps not on the scene; perhaps these embryos are from earlier generations of IVF patients), and also that, though there are insufficient adoptive families for all these new children, we can and will provide them adequate care through an improved foster care system, so that, though their lives will be tougher than many others, they will be glad to have had the chance to live them. Many people would think that there is at least some reason to bring these new children into existence—that it would be at least *permissible* to do so. People's lives will be a little less good *on average*, but nobody in particular will be any worse off, and everyone will be glad they get to live the life they have.

Suppose, now, that we don't have the technology in the last case but are considering whether to begin a research program that will allow us produce all these new people, in this way. In the meantime, we can find adoptive families for all the children these new technologies would help create, but healthcare spending won't be able to keep up completely with the larger population, so the standard of available healthcare will somewhat decline. The result will be that in one hundred years there will be just as many people with decent lives as in the first case, and the average life will be even better than in that case, albeit a little worse than it is now. If we have reason to expand the population in the first case, since that brings more good lives into existence, it looks like we also have reason to do that in this second case, since again we'll have more good lives than the first case, and this time they'll even be better off on average.

So far, so good. But the trouble, as Parfit points out, is that there's nothing to stop us repeating the reasoning process. If it's always at least as good to add more people, when that doesn't mean anyone else would be worse off, and if we can always improve that situation further by improving both the average life and the total number of good lives, then it looks like the best world will be one with as many people as we can make, so long as the cost of making and maintaining those lives still leaves enough for everyone's lives to be just barely worth living. This is Parfit's "repugnant" conclusion—"repugnant" because it seems to imply, implausibly, that when we think about the legacy we leave for future generations we should care much more about how many of them there are than whether they have opportunities to live excellent and interesting lives.

RESPONSES

Philosophers interested in population policy have responded in a variety of way. A few philosophers think we should be willing to accept the repugnant conclusion, even if it is counterintuitive (Huemer 2008). But many people will be uncomfortable with policies that aim to make as many people in the future as possible, caring only that they live halfway-decent lives. They will want to resist Parfit's "repugnant conclusion," that more people are generally better. The way to do this is to reject one or more of the premises of his argument; or to reject the rule of inference that allows us to go from the premises to this conclusion.

One approach is to deny that we should always add more people, when that doesn't make anyone else worse off. We could say, for instance, that it's always wrong to reduce the average level of well-being in the population, even if that's done without reducing any actual person's well-being. That would follow from what is sometimes called "average utilitarianism," the idea that our goal should be to make the average level of well-being as high as possible, without caring how many people enjoy this well-being or how much happiness there is "in total" (Pressman 2015). This principle simply seems wrong, though; it would imply, for instance, that we should prefer to let population dwindle almost down to nothing, if each generation would otherwise be even a little worse off than the last (Parfit 1984). For this reason and others, the total level of well-being seems to matter, alongside the average level.

Another way to stop the process, which leads us to the Repugnant Conclusion, is to deny that it's OK to add people, even with lives worth living, if their lives are not sufficiently good—good enough so that we would not find the prospect of a population where everyone is at this "critical level" repugnant (Kavka 1982; Broome 2004). This avoids the problem, but to many it seems ad hoc or arbitrary, since there is no obvious, principled way to set this level that avoids the problem. Remember that the repugnant conclusion presumes that the lives of the large population are "worth living," so that the people living them would rather have lived than not. The proponent of this response needs to explain why we would ever want to stop adding people whose lives are, in this way, valuable to they themselves, just because their lives are not quite as good as we might hope a new life would be.

A different approach is to focus not on the premises of the argument, but rather the rule of inference. The argument works by comparing three worlds: (1) the world we would get if we refused to add people, whose lives are worse than ours but still worth living; (2) the world we would get if we did add those people; and (3) the world we would get, starting from world (2), if we added even more people who are no worse off. Since world (2) is better than world (1), and world (3) better than world (2), we have to infer that world (3) is better world (1)—and thus, that a bigger population is better, even if everyone is worse off, so long as their lives are still worth living. One way to stop this reasoning is to deny that "betterness" is, as mathematicians would put, "transitive"—meaning that if Y is better than X, and Z is better than Y, then Z is better than X. Here that would mean saying that, even though the world is better the first time we lower the average, just by adding more people, and the world when we get when we add more people to that one is better still, nonetheless world 3 is not actually better than our world. Though some philosophers have defended this idea (Temkin 1987; Rachels 2004), it is hard to account for it. We might think that the worlds in the examples get incrementally better because they have more good things in them—specifically, good lives. If so, then the transitivity of "betterness" here is entailed by the transitivity of "great than or equal to"; since world 2 has more good lives than world 1, and world 3 more than world 2, world 3 has more good lives than world 1—and is, therefore, the better world.

This brings us to deeper issues about how we understand the relationship between our choices and their consequences. Some philosophers would simply deny that we should decide what to do by figuring out how much value our actions will produce. Thinking about things in this "consequentialist" way, they argue, fails to see us as independent separate persons, and in so doing tends to justify treating individual persons as mere means to the end of producing goods like pleasure or preference-satisfaction (Scanlon 1998). If we agree with these "non-consequentialists," then we might not be very worried about the argument to the "repugnant" conclusion, either because we think there is little reason to choose worlds with more happy people (since no existing person can complain if we keep the population the same size); or because, agreeing with judgments Parfit and others make about what to do in the cases that motivate the premises of the Repugnant Conclusion, we deny that these choices are motivated by judgments about goodness to which a requirement of transitivity might apply.

Non-consequentialists, however, still face problems like these in "population" bioethics; that is, they still owe us an account of what decisions we should make when those decisions do not affect existing people, but rather which people exist. Without appeal to claims about the value of different possible scenarios involving different lives, it is at best far from clear how we can think about this.

SUGGESTED READINGS

The case itself comes from, and is discussed in detail, in:
> Parfit, D. 1984, *Reasons and Persons*. Oxford: Clarendon Press.

For a defense "biting the bullet" here, producing large populations of people with lives barely worth living, see:
> Huemer, Michael. 2008. "In Defence of Repugnance." *Mind* 117 (468): 899–933. https://doi.org/10.1093/mind/fzn079.

A recent discussion and defense of the longstanding idea that we should promote the average level of happiness, rather than the total amount:
> Michael Pressman. 2015. "A Defence of Average Utilitarianism." *Utilitas* 27 (4): 389–424. https://doi.org/DOI: 10.1017/S0953820815000072.

For the idea that total well-being matters unless the people added have lives below some "critical level," see:
> Kavka, G.S. 1982. "The Paradox of Future Individuals." *Philosophy and Public Affairs* 11: 93–112.

> Broome, John. 2004. *Weighing Lives*. Oxford: Oxford University Press.

about interests, and notes that it is possible for an abortion that would not be contrary to justice to still be contrary to decency. Whether refusing to aid someone would count as indecent depends on the personal sacrifices providing aid would require. Thomson believes that, although it would not be indecent for a woman to abort a fetus to avoid the normal burdens of a nine-month-long pregnancy, it would be indecent for a woman to abort a fetus in the seventh month simply to avoid postponing a trip abroad. However, Thomson also points out that since we do not enforce Good or even Minimally Decent Samaritan laws generally, it would be unfair to single out pregnant women for enforcement via abortion restrictions.

There is an enormous and rich literature reacting to Thomson's thought experiment. Some critics argue that the Violinist Case fails to show that killing a fetus does not violate its right to life. They concede that unplugging yourself from the Violinist does not violate his right to life but claim that this is because the unplugging is merely an active form of letting die, not a killing, because you (or your agent) are merely withdrawing aid that you are currently providing. If this is correct, then the thought experiment is of no use for defending abortion methods that clearly kill the fetus before or during the process of removal, such as dilation and curettage. It might still be capable of defending abortion methods that merely expel an embryo or fetus from the woman's uterus without fatally damaging its body, such as hysterectomy and the abortion pill, since such methods merely remove support that the woman herself is providing. But some argue that even these methods, unlike unplugging the Violinist, still kill the fetus (Foot 1984). In unplugging yourself from the Violinist, you are merely ceasing to protect him from a pre-existing threat (his illness), but there is no pre-existing threat to the fetus that the woman's gestational assistance is holding at bay—the fetus is merely dependent on the woman. After all, in removing a fish from water, we kill the fish, even if we were the ones maintaining its aquarium (McMahan 2002).

Other critics have argued, against Thomson, that a woman's choice to have sex could give a fetus a right to use her body even if she had taken all reasonable precautions to avoid pregnancy. Suppose that a hunter accidentally shoots someone in the forest, despite having taken all reasonable precautions to avoid this, and that the victim will bleed to death unless they receive an infusion of the hunter's blood. Arguably, the victim still has a right to the hunter's bodily assistance because the hunter caused the victim's need. In reply to this sort of objection, ethicists have argued that the hunter's victim has a right to the hunter's assistance because this assistance is needed to prevent the hunter's earlier act of shooting from causing harm (or additional harm). But the woman (and her partner's) earlier act of creating the fetus will not cause it harm if she refuses to provide the gestational assistance it needs and aborts it. It is not bad for a fetus to exist in utero, even if without her aid it would only exist for a short time (Boonin 2019).

Besides criticisms of Thomson's defense of some abortions against the charge of injustice, there have also been criticisms of Thomson's account of decency or charity and her claim that, even if the interests of fetuses were as morally important as those of the Violinist, carrying a fetus to term would normally be too demanding to be required by decency. One critic has argued that our duties to care for the dependent are, in the first instance, collective duties (Schouten 2017). Since not everyone is fortunate enough to have an intrinsically motivated caregiver, a plan must be devised for distributing responsibilities to individuals to ensure that the collective duty is fully discharged. The problem in the case of fetuses is that, unlike children, the elderly, and the disabled, it is not even possible for anyone else to nurture a fetus in place of a pregnant woman who does not want to continue the pregnancy. Therefore, the burden of caregiving for fetuses unavoidably falls to even unwillingly pregnant women and, although society should do more to lighten the burden of gestation on them than it currently does, it is impossible for that burden to be fully shared.

SUGGESTED READINGS

For the Violinist Case (and one of the most famous articles in bioethics):
> Thomson, Judith Jarvis. 1970. "A Defense of Abortion." *Philosophy & Public Affairs* 1 (1): 47–66.

Presents a defense of abortion similar to Thomson's but with many important modifications:
> Kamm, F. M. 1992. *Creation and Abortion: A Study in Moral and Legal Philosophy*. New York: Oxford University Press.

For the view that even abortions that merely remove the fetus still count as killings:
> Foot, Philippa. 1984. "Killing and Letting Die." In Jay L. Garfield and Patricia Hennessey (eds.), *Abortion: Moral and Legal Perspectives* (pp. 78–87). Amherst, MA: University of Massachusetts Press.

A recent Thomson-style argument relying on the famous *McFall v. Shimp* legal precedent to defend the legality of abortion:

Boonin, David. 2019. *Beyond Roe: Why Abortion Should Be Legal—Even If the Fetus Is a Person.* New York: Oxford University Press.

Defends Thomson's argument against Foot's objection but raises several other objections to Thomson's argument of his own:

McMahan, Jeff. 2002. *The Ethics of Killing: Problems at the Margins of Life.* New York: Oxford University Press.

Argues that, on the assumption that fetuses have full moral status, there is a feminist case to be made for assigning even many unwillingly pregnant women a duty to gestate:

Schouten, Gina. 2017. "Fetuses, Orphans, and a Famous Violinist." *Social Theory and Practice* 43 (3): 637–65.

Discusses indecency and what is distinctive about gestation as a form of assistance:

Little, Margaret Olivia. 1999. "Abortion, Intimacy, and the Duty to Gestate." *Ethical Theory and Moral Practice* 2: 295–312.

9

WHAT WE OWE TO OUR UNBORN CHILDREN

Rescues Easy and Hard

THE CASE

Abortion is one example of a potential maternal–fetal conflict of interest, but conflicts can also arise between a mother and a fetus she intends to carry to term. Since we tend to think that our duties not to do harm are largely insensitive to how much it costs us to avoid doing harm, it is natural to think that a pregnant woman would almost never be justified in engaging in some activity that was likely to damage her fetus's health. Holly Smith challenges that view with the following thought experiment, paraphrased here (Smith 1994):

While driving through a desert you come across a woman who is lying unconscious by the side of the road because she has been bitten by a snake. Whether you have a duty to help depends on how costly helping would be for you. Assume that the nearest hospital is hundreds of miles out of your way, and that this makes helping too costly to be required. (If this sacrifice does not seem substantial enough, increase the costs until it becomes plausible there is no duty to aid.) Nevertheless, you decide to drive her to the hospital anyway. When you arrive at the hospital the doctor warns you that although they will be able to save her life at this hospital, they are not equipped to treat the gangrene in her leg and will have to amputate her limb. But there is

DOI: 10.4324/9781032640525-11

a second hospital that would be able to save both her life and her leg, which is, again, hundreds of miles away. It seems clear that if you had no duty to undertake the first act of assistance, you have no duty to undertake the second.

Now consider a second case. As in the first case, you place the woman in the car and start for the hospital hundreds of miles out of your way. But you soon realize that this route will traumatize her leg to the point where it will need to be amputated when you reach the hospital. There is an alternative route that would avoid traumatizing her leg, but it is hundreds of additional miles out of your way. Do you have a duty to take the longer route, if you attempt to assist the victim at all?

If we accept the common view that our general duty not to do harm to others is "strict" (i.e., largely insensitive to the costs of avoiding doing harm), unlike our general duty to prevent harm to others, then we might expect our answer to Smith's question to be yes, you do have a duty to take the longer route in the second case, despite the extra cost to you. In the first case, in refusing to drive yet another hundred miles, you are merely failing to prevent the loss of the woman's leg, whereas in the second case, in taking the shorter rather than the longer route, you would be *causing* the woman to lose her leg. Yet Smith predicts that our intuition will be that you do *not* have a duty to drive the longer route, and that the same costs that justify your refusal to save the woman's leg in the first case would also justify your taking the shorter route and causing the loss of the woman's leg in the second case. If her prediction is correct, Smith believes that she can use our reactions to this thought experiment to persuade us that pregnant women do not have strict duties to avoid activities that are highly likely to cause non-lethal injuries to fetuses they have no plans to abort, as we'll see below.

RESPONSES

Activities that may endanger the health of the fetus include drinking alcohol, smoking, playing contact sports, working hazardous jobs, participating as a subject in risky clinical research, and taking medicine for one's own health or comfort. Pregnant women who expose their fetuses to high risks of harm while planning to carry it to term tend to attract blame—even from people who believe that abortion is permissible for almost any reason. The law sometimes treats pregnant women harshly as well. Pregnant women who have failed drug tests have been sent to jail to protect the fetus from further risk of harm; they have been charged with child abuse for damage they caused by drinking and using drugs; and children have even sued their mothers for harm caused by acne medication they had taken while pregnant (Scott 2002).

Is this fair to pregnant women? It is initially tempting to think that anyone who believes causing a lethal injury to a fetus (e.g., abortion) is permissible ought to believe that causing non-lethal injuries to fetuses is permissible as well. Suppose that early abortion is permissible because the fetus has no moral status (i.e., because we cannot have any duties *to* the fetus). If we cannot have any duties at all to the fetus, then we obviously cannot have any duties to the fetus not to cause it to suffer a non-lethal injury. Or suppose instead that abortion is permissible because a fetus has only a slight interest in its future (McMahan 2002). It would again appear to follow that non-lethal injury must be permissible too since, even if the fetus's interest in its future is slight, it has a stronger interest in not being deprived of its whole future than in not being deprived of only a certain range of opportunities in that future, which is the result of most non-lethal prenatal injuries.

Yet many people who believe that obtaining an abortion is permissible for almost any reason also believe that exposing a fetus to a high risk of a non-lethal injury is impermissible for almost any reason. Is such a view even coherent? It is because the consequences of non-lethally injuring a fetus will be suffered, not just by the fetus, but also by the child and the adult the fetus will likely become. Even if a fetus lacks moral status entirely or has only a slight interest in its future, the child and the adult clearly have full moral status and a strong interest in access to the range of opportunities that a prenatal injury would deprive them of. So even if we do not have any duties *to* the fetus not to cause it a non-lethal injury, we could still, in virtue of our duties to the child and adult the fetus will likely become, have duties right now *regarding* or *in relation to* that fetus. Abortion is importantly different than non-lethal injury, since it ensures that there will be no child in the future.

Smith acknowledges that there is no straightforward entailment from the permissibility of abortion to the permissibility of exposing a fetus to a high risk of non-lethal injury. Nevertheless, Smith does think that anyone who agrees that pregnant women have no strict duty to continue a pregnancy at all, much less provide an optimal level of gestational assistance, should also, after reflecting on her thought experiment about driving through the desert, arrive at the conclusion that pregnant women are under no strict duty not to cause non-lethal fetal injuries either.

Here's the reasoning. Our general duty not to do harm, unlike our general duty to prevent harm, is largely insensitive to personal costs. Yet in the thought experiment, we are inclined to think that the same costs (driving an extra hundred miles) that would justify a refusal to prevent the loss of the woman's leg in the first case would also justify your *causing* the loss of her leg in the second case. The lesson Smith thinks we should draw from the thought experiment is that we should reject what she labels the Simple Causal View of doing harm. When we cause someone harm as a side-effect of some activity while we are in the *process of providing aid* to that person, causing that harm counts, morally speaking, as merely delivering a less-than-optimal level of aid and is not subject to the strict general duty to avoid doing harm.

Applying this lesson to pregnancy, Smith notes that continuing a pregnancy is a form of aid to the fetus (and the child the fetus is likely to become). If we believe there is no strict duty to provide this assistance, or no strict duty to provide it at an optimal level, then since causing harm in the course of providing this assistance counts merely as a failure to provide an optimal level of aid, there is no strict duty to avoid causing this harm. This doesn't mean that it is never impermissible for pregnant women to cause non-lethal injuries to fetuses they plan to carry to term. But it does mean that whether pregnant women have a duty to avoid causing these injuries is sensitive to the costs of refraining from the activities that would cause those injuries, just as any duties they may have to prevent non-lethal harms to the fetus, such as to accept intrauterine surgery to repair a fetus's spina bifida, are sensitive to the costs of doing or undergoing those things. Thus, assuming it is not too costly to refrain from smoking or drinking (setting aside concerns about addiction) or contact sports, they may still have a duty to do so. But refraining from exposing a fetus to workplace toxins or taking medicine for one's health or comfort that poses a high risk to the fetus might, depending on the details, be too costly to be required.

One obvious objection, which Smith anticipates, is that whereas the driver has no special relation to the snakebite victim, a pregnant woman who plans to carry her fetus to term acquires a special parental responsibility both to protect and to avoid endangering the health of the fetus for the sake of the child the fetus will become. There are difficult questions here about when and why such responsibilities are acquired; e.g., would a pregnant woman who is gestating the fetus as a surrogate or is planning to give it up for adoption acquire the same special responsibility? But assuming a pregnant woman does have such a responsibility, Smith responds that while parental duties may be more demanding than our duties to aid strangers they still fall short of being strict duties. That is, there will be some activities that are dangerous to the fetus but are too valuable to the pregnant woman for her to be required to give them up, even to live up to her duties as a parent.

SUGGESTED READINGS

The case and argument are from:

> Smith, Holly M. 1994. "Fetal-Maternal Conflicts." 1994. In Allen Buchanan and Jules Coleman (eds.), *In Harm's Way: Essays in Honor of Joel Feinberg* (pp. 324–43). Cambridge: Cambridge University Press.

For an argument for the permissibility of causing prenatal injuries that is based on the permissibility of abortion:

> Flanigan, Jessica. 2020. "The Ethics of Prenatal Injury." *Journal of Moral Philosophy*, October, 1–23.

For an argument against the permissibility of abortion based on the impermissibility of causing prenatal injuries:

> Hendricks, Perry. 2019. "Even If the Fetus Is Not a Person, Abortion Is Immoral: The Impairment Argument." *Bioethics* 33 (2): 245–53.

For the view that abortion is permissible because the fetus has only a slight interest in its future:

> McMahan, Jeff. 2002. *The Ethics of Killing: Problems at the Margins of Life.* New York: Oxford University Press.

Argues that causing non-lethal prenatal injury to a fetus is wrong when that fetus will become a child, not just because this would violate a duty to the child, but because this would also violate a duty to the fetus right now:

> Harman, Elizabeth. 1999. "Creation Ethics: The Moral Status of Early Fetuses and the Ethics of Abortion." *Philosophy & Public Affairs* 28 (4): 310–24.

10

IS IT BAD TO BE DISABLED, I?
The Case of Cara and Daisy

THE CASE

Many people who have talked or read about disability will have heard neologisms like "handi-capable" or "differently abled." The idea behind these terms has come to be called *disability pride*: the conviction that disabilities like achondroplasia, paraplegia, or blindness are identities to be celebrated, not tragic medical conditions to be pitied and fixed. Philosophers sympathetic to disability pride have defended what has come to be called the *mere-difference* view of the relation between disability and well-being, arguing that the bodily differences characteristic of disability are not always or necessarily bad for disabled people (Barnes 2014). Proponents of the alternative *detrimental difference* view argue that it must be in some way worse to be deaf, or paraplegic, or otherwise disabled, since it is so clearly morally *wrong* for one person to cause another person to become disabled (McMahan 2005). What could make it wrong, except that it is harmful, that it makes that person worse off than they otherwise would have been?

Elizabeth Barnes has developed a series of examples that illustrate these issues effectively (Barnes 2014). The first case raises a problem for the pro-disability "mere difference" view; the second points to a solution; the third raises problems for that solution.

DOI: 10.4324/9781032640525-13

First, she has us consider Cara and Daisy. Cara is a disability advocate with a six-month-old daughter, Daisy, who does not have a disability. Cara wants to express her positive attitude towards disability and strengthen the disability community. She decides to seek a largely painless procedure for Daisy which will give her a disability for the rest of her life (Barnes does not say which, but we can assume it is a condition that does not cause pain or radically restrict opportunity—blindness, say, or very short stature). Barnes believes that most of us would think that Cara has done something wrong here. We will thus be tempted to take the *detrimental difference* view, since it seems like the best explanation of Cara's wrongdoing is that she harms Daisy, or makes her worse off, by inducing the disability.

Barnes, however, asks us to consider a modification of this case, in hopes of showing that we can judge Cara here without committing to the bad-difference view of disability. Imagine instead, next, that Cara is as or more concerned with justice for people with same-sex orientation as with justice for the disabled. To express her commitment to this cause, and strengthen the LGBTQ community, she decides to seek an innovative procedure for Daisy that will ensure she grows up to be gay (assume, contrary to actual fact, that procedures like this are safe and effective; see Chapter 42 for discussion). Barnes believes that we will judge that she has done something wrong here, even though there is nothing inherently harmful about being gay. The best explanation of this, she thinks, is that we shouldn't make this kind of profound change to a person before they are old enough to understand and consent to it. (Similar points apply, she thinks, in the real world case of "sex assignment" surgeries for intersex children.) If, however, what explains the wrongness of Daisy's action in the second case is this "non-interference" principle, then it seems that this may be what explains it in the first case as well, the case that involves disability. If so, then critics of the mere difference view may be wrong to insist that our judgments about the wrongness of causing disability commit us to seeing disability as always or in general a bad thing.

That said, Barnes recognizes that this non-interference principle can be challenged by yet another modification of the original case. Imagine now that Daisy is born with a disability, which Cara can remove with a relatively painless procedure. Doing so will profoundly change Daisy in a way that will affect how she sees herself throughout her life. Yet, many of us will tend to think that this is a good thing for Cara to do. But if causing disability is wrong, while causing non-disability isn't, but both involve equal kinds and degrees of non-consensual interference, then it looks like the interference principle does not explain what is going on in these cases after all. Instead, it looks like the difference is that taking Daisy's disability away makes her better off, while making her disabled (or gay, or not gay) would not. This points back to the detrimental difference view.

RESPONSES

Barnes herself has two kinds of responses to this last challenge; critics have not been persuaded by either one. A first response is to point out that we can think that it's wrong to cause disabilities even if we don't think that disabilities are always and in general bad for us. Making someone disabled is risky, likely to make them worse off than they would have been if they weren't disabled. But, as critics point out, this doesn't seem to be much a defense of the mere-difference view. If disabled people face greater risks no matter what—say, because even in a good society they are more vulnerable to misfortune—then this looks like something that is generally bad or detrimental about disability (Vuko and Wundisch, 2015). If, on the other hand, the reason not to make babies like Daisy disabled is that they will be at risk of harm from social prejudice and stigma, then the point is irrelevant to the mere-difference debate—which is about whether disability is good or bad for us per se, not about whether it is actually bad or risky to be disabled in an ableist society.

Another response here on behalf of the mere-difference view is to say that we only think that it is good to "cure" or change disabled people because of internalized stigma around disability (it is easy to imagine a deaf person saying this, for instance, about their deafness). This means that many people who start with strongly pro-disability intuitions may not be convinced by the concerns raised in the Cara and Daisy case. But, it's not clear that this takes away all of the philosophical force of objections to the mere-difference view rooted in the appearance of cause–cure asymmetries (Kahane and Savulescu 2016). Many people, philosophers and otherwise, will come to this debate not already knowing what to think about mere difference, but pretty sure that it is usually bad to cause, but good to remove or prevent, most if not all disabilities. If the mere-difference view implies that causing and curing are on a par for many or most disabilities, then these arguments give these people good reason to resist accepting it, even if they don't necessarily give existing proponents of the mere-difference view good reason to give it up.

Even if we are convinced by critics to reject Barnes's defense of the mere difference view, that doesn't mean that we have to accept the detrimental-difference view instead. There are other arguments we might make that disabilities are not always or in general bad for you. For one thing, it just seems hard to generalize about the effects of disability in general or particular disabilities: having a disability often makes such a big difference to how a life goes that it may be hard or impossible to say how well that life would have gone without it (Campbell and Stramondo 2017). And even if we accept the detrimental-difference view, it's not obvious that we have to give up on disability positive language or on the core claims and concepts of the disability movement. Even if disability might still be a little harmful in an ideal world, the disadvantages disabled people face in the actual world might be overwhelmingly the result of exclusion and stigma (see Chapter 13 for discussion of this "social model of disability"). If so, then it seems clear that pity wouldn't be the right response to actual disability disadvantage—but, rather, moral outrage (Stramondo 2010). And disabled people might still feel pride in their disability— say, in their skill in adapting their body to a hostile world—whatever they think about whether they could or would have been better off if they didn't have to adapt in the first place.

SUGGESTED READINGS

For an argument that disability must be bad, since it is wrong to cause disability, see:

> McMahan, Jeff. 2005. "Causing Disabled People to Exist and Causing People to Be Disabled." *Ethics* 116 (1): 77–99. https://doi.org/10.1086/454367.

For the Cara and Daisy case, as a defense of the mere difference view against McMahan's objection:

> Barnes, Elizabeth. 2014. "Valuing Disability, Causing Disability." *Ethics* 125 (1): 88–113. https://doi.org/10.1086/677021.

Two critical responses to Barnes, objecting both to the mere-difference view and her defense of it:

Andric, Vuko, and Joachim Wundisch. 2015. "Is It Bad to Be Disabled? Adjudicating Between the Mere-Difference and Bad-Difference Views of Disability." *Journal of Ethics & Social Philosophy* 9 (3).

Kahane, Guy, and Julian Savulescu. 2016. "Disability and Mere Difference." *Ethics* 126 (3): 774–88. https://doi.org/10.1086/684709.

For a comprehensive discussion of subtleties around disability and well-being, and particularly the difficulty of contrasting a person's life with a disability with how their life would be without it, see:

Campbell, Stephen M., and Joseph A. Stramondo. 2017. "The Complicated Relationship of Disability and Well-Being." *Kennedy Institute of Ethics Journal* 27: 1–33. https://doi.org/10.1353/ken.2017.0014.

On what attitudes are appropriate in response to disability:

Stramondo, Joseph A. 2010. "How an Ideology of Pity Is a Social Harm to People with Disabilities." *Social Philosophy Today* 26 (July): 121–34. https://doi.org/10.5840/socphiltoday20102610.

IS IT BAD TO BE DISABLED, II?
Adaptive Preference?

THE CASE

Is it bad to have a disability, like deafness or paraplegia? Many people think so, before experiencing these conditions (and, as we just saw in Chapter 10, some others think they have a good argument for this). But those who become disabled, and those who always have been, often claim that it is not so bad to have even apparently very serious disabilities—perhaps, for some disabilities, not worse on the whole than not having being disabled at all. Disabled people value the lives they build, and the distinctive capacities they use to build them. The writer Helen Keller, both deaf and blind, describes the great compensating advantages of learning to rely on the senses she had:

> My world is built of touch-sensations, devoid of physical color and sound; but without color and sound, it breathes and throbs with life. Every object is associated in my mind with tactual qualities which, combined in countless ways, give me a sense of power, of beauty, or of incongruity: for with my hands I can feel the comic as well as the beautiful in the outward appearance of things. Remember that you, dependent on your sight, do not realize how many things are tangible.
>
> (2003: 11)

DOI: 10.4324/9781032640525-14

It seems clear that some disabled people—perhaps, Keller herself—would not *prefer* a life where they are rid of their disability. This in itself looks like evidence that those disabilities, at least, are not bad after all. Who, we might ask, is in a better position to know what makes a life good or bad, better or worse, than the person who lives it?

Those who doubt that these disabilities are "mere differences" (perhaps, for the reason discussed in Chapters 10 or 11) respond, reasonably, that we cannot infer that something is good for someone, just because they think it is, or want or *prefer* that it occur. Real-world examples abound ("Stockholm syndrome" in kidnap victims; "false consciousness" or ideological adaptation to injustice). But the classic illustration is a very ancient sort of thought experiment, the fable of the fox and the grapes.

Here, a fox comes across a juicy bunch of grapes. But they are just out of reach; he tries and tries to reach them, but eventually gives up. To console himself, he says: "Why am I wasting time looking for grapes? They are too sour for foxes anyway." In the version of the story that matters to us, the fox hasn't just changed his mind about how sour grapes actually are; rather, he has changed his *values* or *preferences*, such that he no longer wants grapes—and he made this change only because he cannot have them.

We are invited to conclude that this change in preference does not mean the fox is really just as well off without the grapes; even though he really doesn't want them anymore, his new preferences are too *adaptive* for reduced ambitions to be truly authentic (Elster 1983). And, we are supposed to say the same about the indifference of a deaf person to music, or a blind person to the sight of a sunset: if they do not care that they miss out on those things, that is because they think of them as a sort of "sour grape," something they would want, if they could have it, and therefore something they would be better off having, if they could have it.

RESPONSES

We can respond to this use of the fable of the fox in two ways: by rejecting the claim that the fox's preference is irrational or otherwise problematic, or rejecting the analogy between the preferences of the fox and the preferences of people with disabilities. Everything depends on what (if anything) is supposed to be wrong with the fox's "adaptive" preference.

One thought is that the problem is that the fox changes his mind about grapes out of pure frustration, not because he has thought about what he really likes and decided that grapes are just not for him (Elster 1983). It doesn't look like disabled people normally adjust their goals and ambitions in life by thinking hard about it, rather than just by getting used to their new life and its opportunities. It's not clear, though, that preference adaptation is a problem any time it happens without really thinking about it (Bovens 1992). Disabled or not, we often adjust our priorities subconsciously as we get a better sense of what we are in a position to achieve in life. So, it looks like this procedural test won't tell us whether there's a distinctive problem with adapting to disability.

A totally different kind of approach focuses not on the processes that produce problematically "adaptive" preferences, like the fox's, but on whether the preferences are, in some sense, objectively the right ones (Nussbaum 2001; Khader 2011). The fox is made worse off when he gives up on grapes because grapes are just, really, delicious, whether he thinks so or not. In that case, giving up on them is giving up something good, because you can't get it. That seems like a bad thing to have to do, and when you have to do it, it seems you are worse off.

Notice, though, that this way of thinking about adaptive preference may not help us much if we want to know whether it is bad to be disabled. We would already need to know whether the activities and opportunities that particular disabled people miss out on are objectively good or bad, *for them*, to know whether we should take seriously their claim that their life is going fine, even though they don't have these things in it. But that's exactly what's in dispute (and, as we saw in Chapter 11, difficult to determine, not least because people's interests often shift legitimately as their abilities do).

This brings us to a deeper question, about how we should understand what other people say about what they want, and how their lives are going. The adaptive preference move is a doubting move: it tells us to doubt others, when they make a claim about what they need to leave a good life. Perhaps instead we should trust people when they say things like this about themselves (Barnes 2009). Not completely or always—sometimes, someone is being insincere, puffing or producing false bravado when they say they are fine. This is how we might imagine the fox with the grapes—he *hasn't* really stopped liking grapes, just stopped *saying* that he does. This might be true of many disabled people, who say they don't want things they can't have—maybe sometimes they are only trying to maintain or defend their dignity, or make a bigger political point. But then again it might not be—they might be making a political point or defending their dignity *by* reporting just exactly how they feel. If they are being sincere in describing what a good life means to them, it seems we would need a strong argument indeed to contradict them.

SUGGESTED READINGS

Hellen Keller's description of her experience of touch is from:
> Keller, Helen (2003) "The Seeing Hand." In *The World I Live In*. New York: New York Review of Books Classics.

The fable of the fox itself is ancient, probably Greek; it comes into the philosophical literature on adaptive preference in:
> Elster, J. (1983). *Sour Grapes: Studies in the Subversion of Rationality*. New York: Cambridge University Press.

For the argument that legitimate preference shifts can be unplanned and even unconscious see:
> Bovens, L. (1992). Sour Grapes and Character Planning. *The Journal of Philosophy*, *89* (2), 57–78. https://doi.org/10.2307/2027152

For two versions of the idea that preference shifts are problematic only when they lead to preferring things what is not objectively preferable, see:
> Nussbaum, M. "Adaptive Preferences and Women's Options." *Economics and Philosophy*, 17 (1): 67–88. https://doi.org/10.1017/S0266267101000153.

> Khader, S. J. (2011). *Adaptive Preferences and Women's Empowerment*. Oxford: Oxford University Press.

For discussion of reasons for and against deference to the testimony of disabled people, in this context:
> Barnes, E. (2009). Disability and Adaptive Preference. *Philosophical Perspectives*, *23*: 1–22. https://www.jstor.org/stable/40658392

12

MORBIDITY VERSUS MORTALITY
The QALY Trap

THE CASE

Whether and how disability, and disease, are bad for us, matters practically: for reproductive decisions, for clinical decision-making, and maybe for health policy, too. To see how, suppose you were a health policymaker, trying to decide which cancer treatment to develop and produce. One treatment delays death from cancer by five years, but has terrible side effects, so that these five years are often miserable. The other only extends life by four years, but it has few or no side effects. Which should you invest in? Many people would say the second treatment: mortality or quantity of life is not the only thing that matters in health policy; morbidity/quality of life matters too. It turns out, though, that standard ways of accounting for this judgment in health economics put policymakers in a bind.

If policymakers are going to responsibly consider both extending and improving life, they need some systematic way of comparing mortality benefits and morbidity benefits. Economists and policymakers devised an elegant solution here (Zeckhauser and Shepard 1976; Weinstein and Stason 1977). Suppose we start with the idea that health policy should try to prevent premature deaths, because every life is valuable to the person living it. Policymakers should make choices that try to maximize or increase the number of life years in

DOI: 10.4324/9781032640525-15

the population (though see Chapter 35, on ventilator allocation, for concerns about even this measure). But as the cancer drug case suggests, we shouldn't care as much about extending life if the years we add are worse to live. If you would rather live four years mostly in a state of relatively good health than five years experiencing certain debilitating drug side effects, then it looks like you think those five years are worth less than the four years the other drug gives you; thus, that they are less than 4/5 or 80 percent as good. Policymakers, so the thought goes, can reason the same way, adjusting the value of the life years their policy choices are supposed produce by a factor, called a quality weight, that tries to capture how good those years are to live.

This is an elegant solution, allowing policymakers to combine mortality and morbidity into a single measure, the QALY (quality-adjusted life year), which their policies can then aim to increase or "maximize." This single measure, however, is what lays the infamous "QALY trap" (Ubel et al. 2000).

For suppose, now, that our decision is not about what cancer drug to develop, but about how to distribute a scarce lifesaving resource, like a vaccine in a pandemic. Now compare two populations of equal size, one with many disabled people and another with few. Suppose that these population are equally susceptible to the pandemic disease itself, and that the vaccine is equally likely to prevent death from the disease in both groups. It looks like we can get more QALYs by giving the vaccine to the healthy population. This is not just because life expectancy may already be higher in the non-disabled population, so that we get more life years by preventing pandemic deaths. Even if all the disabilities are largely irrelevant to lifespan, they can still be expected to make life worse (according to the QALY framework). Every disabled life is therefore worth less, literally worth fewer QALYs, than the life of a non-disabled or fully healthy person. That means that a policy that tries to produce as many QALYs as possible will tend to give lifesaving resources to non-disabled populations over disabled ones (Harris 1987).

RESPONSES

To many, this looks like an unacceptable implication: an unfair and unjust kind of disability discrimination. Critics and defenders of the QALY framework have diagnosed the problem here in different ways.

One natural response here is to dispute the claims about disability and quality of life that create the problem in the first place. QALY frameworks tend to be constructed by surveying healthcare professionals, or the public at large, about how bad it would be to be, for example, deaf or paraplegic. Disabled people point out that the people asked about how bad these states have never experienced them, and thus are not really in a position to know (Barnes 2009). If disabled people do not actually have lower quality of life, then they get just as many QALYs when their lives are saved, as non-disabled people do.

Per Chapter 11, it is a matter of controversy whether and when this "mere difference" view of disability is correct. However, the "QALY trap" problem would remain in some cases even if we thought many disabilities, like deafness or paraplegia, do not necessarily detract from quality of life. For one thing, many disabled people would agree that, contingently, social discrimination does make it worse to be (for instance) deaf or paraplegic than not to be. To be sure, it is unclear whether this purely "social" sort of "morbidity" should be counted here (Persad 2019). But some other disabilities seem to involve forms of suffering or disadvantage which, though probably worsened by social injustice, would still be substantial without it. Think of chronic migraines, or other conditions that cause significant suffering no matter how well socially accommodated and medically well-treated their sufferers may be. These cases still set a trap for policymakers who want to maximize QALYs; still, the way to do this would be to save the life of a person who suffers less over the life of someone who suffers more.

Another approach to the problem focuses on the unfairness of punishing people who are already—per hypothesis—worse off, because of their disability. Philosophers have argued, in this context and others, that we should be more concerned with benefiting people who are already worse off (John et al., 2017). The idea, then, would be that even if saving the life of a person with a painful medical condition would produce less QALYs, we have special compensating reason to do so anyway, because that person deserves more of our care and attention than someone who is in the same level of mortal danger now but has had the chance to live a better life on the whole. Depending on how much we prioritize the disadvantaged, this may or may not avoid the QALY trap entirely. It does so, however, at the price of singling out some disabled people as objects for pity (or, at least, special concern or compassion), perhaps running contrary to some of the motivations and arguments behind disability pride and the mere difference view (again, see Chapter 10).

A final, more radical line of response is to reject the idea of comparing mortality and morbidity altogether (Harris 1987). The thought here is that saving a life always takes priority over improving a life. It is never OK to let someone die simply to allow someone else to live better. This can sound plausible when we consider cases where death is imminent and certain—as in battlefield triage (or, some argue, other emergency situations—see Chapter 35). But it is less clear that we can safely ignore all considerations of morbidity in contexts where effects on mortality are more remote, or uncertain. Policymakers sometimes have to decide whether an increase in the chances of death for abstracted persons or populations can be justified by an increase in the chances of reducing non-death harms. To say that we should not leave an identified, present person to imminent death does not imply that we can never take actions that increase the risk of death to accomplish other goals, like improving life.

SUGGESTED READINGS

Some of the first comprehensive discussions of the QALY can be found in:

Zeckhauser, Richard, and Donald Shepard. 1976. "Where Now for Saving Lives?" *Law and Contemporary Problems* 40 (4): 5. https://doi.org/10.2307/1191310.

Weinstein, Milton C, and William B. Stason. 1977. "Foundations of Cost-Effectiveness Analysis for Health and Medical Practices." *New England Journal of Medicine* 296 (13): 716–21. https://doi.org/10.1056/NEJM197703312961304.

Influential early discussions of the "QALY Trap" include:

Harris, J. 1987. "QALYfying the Value of Life." *Journal of Medical Ethics* 13 (3): 117–23. https://doi.org/10.1136/jme.13.3.117.

Ubel, Peter A., Erik Nord, Marthe Gold, Paul Menzel, Jose-Luis Pinto Prades, and Jeff Richardson. 2000. "Improving Value Measurement in Cost-Effectiveness Analysis." *Medical Care* 38 (9). https://doi.org/10.1097/00005650-200009000-00003.

For helpful discussion of common survey methodologies for measuring health-related quality of life, see:

Whitehead, Sarah J., and Shehzad Ali. 2010. "Health Outcomes in Economic Evaluation: The QALY and Utilities." *British Medical Bulletin* 96 (1): 5–21. https://doi.org/10.1093/bmb/ldq033.

For discussion of the "mere difference" view of disability see:

Barnes, Elizabeth. 2009. "Disability, Minority, and Difference." *Journal of Applied Philosophy* 26 (4): 337–55. https://doi.org/10.1111/j.1468-5930.2009.00443.x.

On the idea that "social" causes of disadvantage should be discounted in QALY-weighting, see:

Persad, Govind. 2019. "Considering Quality of Life While Repudiating Disability Injustice: A Pathways Approach to Setting Priorities." *Journal of Law, Medicine and Ethics* 47 (2): 294–303. https://doi.org/10.1177/1073110519857285.

For the idea that giving priority to the worst off can help us avoid or at least mitigate the QALY trap, see:

John, Tyler M., Joseph Millum, and David Wasserman. 2017. "How to Allocate Scarce Health Resources Without Discriminating Against People with Disabilities." *Economics and Philosophy* 33 (2): 161–86. https://doi.org/10.1017/S0266267116000237.

For an argument that, in the context of pandemics, we should ignore improving lives in favor of saving "life years":

Wasserman, David, Govind Persad, and Joseph Millum. 2020. "Setting Priorities Fairly in Response to Covid-19: Identifying Overlapping Consensus and Reasonable Disagreement." *Journal of Law and the Biosciences* 7 (1): 1–12. https://doi.org/10.1093/jlb/lsaa044.

13

WHAT MAKES A DISABILITY?
The Counterfactual Test

THE CASE

Whether or not disability is necessarily bad for us, people with disabilities like blindness or paraplegia often have substantial difficulties navigating their actual environments. A major debate in disability bioethics concerns what explains those difficulties. A *social* model of disability has us see disadvantage due to disability as, primarily, a consequence of social decisions, like the decision to build buildings without ramps and elevators, or to communicate information using text unreadable to people without sight (UPIAS 1976). This is to be contrasted with a *medical* model of disability, which understands disadvantage as deriving from the condition itself. The distinction between these models seems significant, since they orient us in different ways regarding how best to address the problems disabled people face. The social model will tend to support political action as a remedy, changing social norms and the built environment to be less exclusionary of people with real or perceived bodily difference. The medical model will tend to support modifying those bodily differences themselves, "curing" or treating the underlying condition to allow more "normal" functioning.

DOI: 10.4324/9781032640525-16

These two views are probably best understood as models or ways of representing particular disabilities, rather than universal theses about disability itself. That is, some disabilities (those involving severe suffering or intrinsic cognitive limitation, say) may fit the medical model better, whilst some may be a better fit for the social model (behavioral differences like those characteristic of mild autism; paraplegia). In some cases, it may be hard to tell. How, then, do we determine whether any given condition better fits a social model, or a medical model?

Anita Silvers (1998) suggests that we use a thought experiment as a test—specifically, for whether disability disadvantage is a result of an oppressed or subordinated social position, rather than the natural state of things. In this thought experiment we turn the tables, imagining that the bodily difference in question were the overwhelming norm in the population. She calls this "historical counterfactualizing."

To illustrate this idea Silvers cites the real-world example of Het Dorp, a village in the Netherlands constructed for people with mobility impairments like paraplegia. Het Dorp, as described by sociologist Irving Zola (1982), is a society where the built environment and social norms are geared for people with paraplegia, so that there is no disadvantage to moving around in a wheelchair rather than on two feet. To show that (say) paraplegia is a social rather than natural disadvantage, we're meant to imagine how the whole world would and could be built, if people with paraplegia had the social power to make the world fit for them. If that world, like Het Dorp, would put paraplegics on an equal playing field with non-paraplegics, then we can conclude that disadvantage due to paraplegia is a result of a different (and, in Silvers' view, discriminatory) social choice.

RESPONSES

We can raise various concerns about this way of using counterfactual reasoning to determine when a social model of disability applies to a given condition.

For one thing, the worlds it has us imagine are very different ones than ours, worlds where disabilities presently very rare are instead quite common. This also means that conditions of non-disability now quite common would be rare, in ways that would make a difference to the way the world would be put together. Much money could be saved, for instance, by lowering ceilings in buildings, from ten feet to six. That short people would be better off in this world does not seem to be a powerful argument that height too is a social construct, and certainly not an argument that high ceilings are an example of structural ableism.

Silvers might respond that even though height itself is no social construct, being "short" or "tall," smaller or bigger than socially salient standard of height, might be—that how vertical extension affects functioning is profoundly and directly determined by social choices, even if that extension itself is not. Still, the point remains that simply pointing out that things might have been constructed otherwise does not show that the way they are now constructed is morally objectionable. Society, unavoidably, will be constructed in ways that advantage some abilities and disadvantage others. The question is when this is fair. The original counterfactual test, the test that turns the tables on non-disabled people, does not seem to tell us. That it would be possible for society to disable different people than it does now does not (as Silvers would surely agree) show that it would be just or fair to do so.

What Silvers really seems to have in mind here is not so much turning the tables on non-disabled people as asking for a seat at the table for everyone. This, and the example of Het Dorp, suggest a modified counterfactual test: instead of asking whether a given trait would be a disadvantage if everybody had it, we ask whether there is a world where it is not a disadvantage to anybody, even though *somebody* has it—whether it is possible to accommodate it as a matter of *universal design* (Center for Universal Design, 1997). Many accessibility measures have this feature. So, for instance, ramps help people in wheelchairs, but also people wheeling suitcases or pulling handcarts. Even condition-specific accommodations like braille text in public spaces can benefit others, both giving them assurance that they will be accommodated if and when they become disabled, and giving them the benefit of disabled people's participation in public life.

Compared to the original counterfactual test, this one is less likely to produce false positives for disability injustice—high ceilings accommodate everyone, tall and short alike. But it also seems likely to miss many important cases of disability injustice. Sometimes accommodation is expensive, and specific in its benefits, to the point that it likely literally costs us more, in economic terms, than we gain by doing it.

It is unlikely, for instance, that providing round-the-clock health aides to disabled professionals always unleashes more economic potential than it consumes. Certainly, we can imagine cases of very expensive accommodation (for instance, the brain-scanning communication technology discussed in Chapter 14). And some accommodations are helpful to some disabled people but harmful to others (Shakespeare 2006)—bright lights in a classroom might help someone with low vision, but be harder to handle for someone with migraines. In these cases, it may be that the presence of a disability in a society entails that someone must be disadvantaged by it: the disabled person themselves, if they are not accommodated, or those who might have used these resources in another way, if they are. Yet, it is still a choice, in these cases, not to accommodate disability, and it may sometimes be an unjust choice: sometimes we ought to incur real costs to accommodate people who need distinctive kinds of accommodation.

An alternative approach to both versions of the counterfactual test, suggested by Silvers' language of *historical* counterfactualizing, focuses more on what actually happened, in the history of disability, than what might have happened (Stramondo 2020). The thought here is that what matters most morally is not the mere fact that that society might handle a given disability better or more generously than it does, but rather that often societies fail to do so as a result of a history of manifestly unjust stigma and prejudice about disability. This is often what is really at stake in the claim that a given trait is a social construct. Those who insist that gender or race are social constructs rarely go on to approve of the way these social categories are constructed! And this can seem to be a good test, too, for when it is an injustice that one group is worse off than another: explaining, for instance, how the legacy of racial injustice (see Chapters 29, 34, 37) in the United States and elsewhere makes contemporary inequalities between racial groups unjust.

There is indeed a terrible, sometimes gruesome, and ongoing history of prejudice, stigma, and abuse against disabled people in much of the world. Surely much disability disadvantage is explained by the effects of past and present wrongs of these kinds. Still, there is reason to doubt that a historical test accurately identifies all the cases where we think someone is unfairly disadvantaged because of how society responds to their body (Aas 2020). This is, first, because there may be some cases of fully new disability injustice, where a condition not previously recognized or stigmatized as a disability becomes so (think of ADHD here, or chronic fatigue syndrome). More deeply, however, it seems clear that we cannot always understand why historical wrongs were wrong, without knowing what was owed to disabled people at the time. If so, then this historical test will not be applicable unless we have a deeper criterion by which to judge history itself.

So, none of these tests—neither Silvers' original counterfactual test, nor a modified, universalizing, version of it, nor a historical alternative—provides a complete way of telling us when a "social model" properly applies to a given disability. To be clear, that doesn't mean that the social model is wrong, that there are at least some cases where a disabled person is disadvantaged just because of the state of their society, not because of the state of their body. Sometimes something is obviously true, even if we do not know exactly why it is true. Even then, it is worth figuring out.

SUGGESTED READINGS

For an early, influential statement of the social model of disability—made initially by activists, rather than theorists—see:

UPIAS. 1976. *Fundamental Principles of Disability*. London: Union of the Physically Impaired Against Segregation. https://disabledpeoplesarchive.com/fundamental-principles-of-disability-union-of-the-physically-impaired-against-segregation/.

Silvers herself introduces the counterfactual test in:

Silvers, Anita. 1998. "Formal Justice." In Anita Silvers, David T. Wasserman, and Mary B. Mahowald (eds.), *Disability, Difference, Discrimination: Perspectives on Justice in Bioethics and Public Policy*. Lanham, MD: Rowman & Littlefield.

For a detailed description of Het Dorp, see the following, by a sociologist who is disabled themselves:

Zola Irving Kenneth. 1982. *Missing Pieces: A Chronicle of Living with a Disability*. Philadelphia: Temple University Press. https://archive.org/details/missingpieces00irvi.

An overview of the idea of "universal" design:

Center for Universal Design. 1997. "The Principles of Universal Design, Version 2.0." https://universaldesign.ie/what-is-universal-design/the-7-principles/.

And for some challenges to the possibility of fully "universal" design:

Shakespeare, Tom. 2006. *Disability Rights and Wrongs*. London: Routledge.

For the historical version of the counterfactual test, on which what matters is whether a disability is detrimental because of contingent historical injustice, see:

Stramondo, Joseph A. 2020. "The Right to Assistive Technology." *Theoretical Medicine and Bioethics* 41 (5–6): 247–71. https://doi.org/10.1007/s11017-020-09527-8.

And for criticism of the historical interpretation, arguing that it presupposes a non-historical account of disability in justice:

Aas, Sean. 2020. "Disability, Society, and Personal Transformation." *Journal of Moral Philosophy* 18: 1–26. https://doi.org/10.1163/17455243-BJA10060.

Arguments that communication with these patients can and should be restored can be found in:

Fins, J. (2015). *Rights Come to Mind: Brain Injury, Ethics, and the Struggle for Consciousness*. New York: Cambridge University Press.

Peterson, A., Mintz, K., and Owen, A. M. (2022). "Unlocking the Voices of Patients with Severe Brain Injury." *Neuroethics* 15 (1). https://doi.org/10.1007/s12152-022-09492-0

For the debate between precautionary and expected-value approaches to allocating resources, to patients with disorders of consciousness, see (respectively):

Braddock, M. (2017). "Should We Treat Vegetative and Minimally Conscious Patients as Persons?" *Neuroethics* 10, 267–80. https://doi.org/10.1007/s12152-017-9309-8

Peterson, A., S. Aas, & D. Wasserman (2021). "What Justifies the Allocation of Health Care Resources to Patients with Disorders of Consciousness?" *American Journal of Bioethics Neuroscience* 12 (2–3): 127–39.

15

DECIDING FOR DISABILITY

The Ashley Treatment

THE CASE

Does every child have a right to grow into an adult, passing through puberty and developing the characteristics humans normally do, as they get older? Ashley X, a real girl born in 1997, did not get to do so. Ashley was born with a very severe cognitive impairment, which left her unable to walk, sit up, or even roll over in bed on her own. Nonetheless, she is responsive and has a mutually caring relationship with her family, who call her their "pillow angel." After observing early signs of puberty when she was a small child, Ashley's parents became concerned that it would be difficult to take care of a full-sized and fully developed adult with cognitive capacities more typical of a newborn infant.

On the advice of their physicians, Ashley's parents opted for a series of procedures that would prevent physical growth and reproductive development. They included high-dose estrogen therapy to prevent growth, a hysterectomy to support this therapy and prevent future menstruation, and breast-bud removal to prevent the development of adult-sized breasts, believed likely to be an impediment to helping Ashley move around in her wheelchair. These procedures were approved by a committee of ethicists at the institution where they were

DOI: 10.4324/9781032640525-19

performed; this committee found that "the potential long terms benefits to Ashley herself outweighed the risks" (quoted in WPAS 2007). Her parents later reported that the procedures were successful—five years later, at the age of 14 or 15, she had not developed adult sexual characteristics or grown significantly larger than she had been when the "treatment" began (Edwards 2011).

Ashley's doctors published the medical details of her case (without identifying her or her family) soon thereafter (Gunther and Diekema 2006); this immediately produced significant public outcry, and heated discussion in bioethics and disability studies. That outcry, however, has not stopped treatments from like this being used since, perhaps hundreds of times, as doctors have become more comfortable with these procedures in these cases and parents have come to think that their severely disabled children could also benefit.

RESPONSES

The Ashley "treatment" raises numerous ethical issues. Many people are concerned with this infringement on Ashley's right to "bodily integrity" (WPAS 2007). This, however, looks more like a name for the problem than an analysis of it. Medical procedures intervene in the body all the time. The question is when and why this is justified. Some might suggest that the problem here is a lack of consent. This, however, also appears misguided. Ashley seemed to have no special objection to this procedure, and in any case as a severely disabled young person she cannot give *informed consent* to any treatment, no matter how beneficial or well-justified. Generally, parents or other surrogates are empowered to make decisions about medical care in cases where the patient cannot make them herself. Thus, the main question here seems to be this: whether the parents acted rightly in consenting to this intervention, on Ashley's behalf.

A related concern is that this intervention stops the "natural course" of development for children like Ashley—so many medical treatments are about restoring biological normality (see Chapter 10), it can seem perverse to intentionally introduce a developmentally abnormal state. Yet, on reflection, it is far from clear that allowing bodies to develop "normally" is important in itself. The relevant notion of normality is hard to understand—disease is normal in the sense of "natural," part of the ordinary order of things, and indeed some diseases (tooth decay, arteriosclerosis) are "normal" in the sense of common or typical, too. Most people who think about the moral importance of normality think that abnormality matters only when it is *harmful*, in some other sense, to the person in question (Wakefield 1992). So the question here seems to be really whether the procedure would harm Ashley, not whether it produces "abnormality" as opposed to "normality."

Not being harmful is not enough, of course. Most physicians, and particularly most pediatricians, would be reluctant to treat patients unless the patients themselves *benefit* from the treatment. Some argue, however, that in Ashley's case her parents were the real beneficiaries, since the point was to make it easier for *them* to care for her (Coleman 2007). This argument, however, seems to suppose that Ashley's interests are totally independent of her parents, and that her parents will give just as good care whether she gets the intervention or not. That is hardly obvious. If Ashley can get better care as a result of the procedure that itself is, in this way at least, better for her. More deeply, if she is part of a tight family unit; arguably her parents' good is part of her own, much as her good is part of her parents'.

Other critics of the procedure are more sympathetic to parents like Ashley's, allowing that they are genuinely motivated by concern for their daughter's interests. In particular, they seem to have genuinely thought that the kind of still-childlike body these procedures would produce for her would suit her permanently child-like abilities better than the body that would develop "naturally." Still, some argue that the fact that her parents saw her, in their words, as a "pillow angel," a perpetual infant, rather than a human who will live for decades, may have actually distorted their conception of what is best for her. This may lead the parents to underplay her interests in living out her version of a complete, adult human life—interests in experiencing a larger and more developed body, perhaps, or simply in seeing what it is like to grow (Kittay 2011).

Critics have also been concerned about what this procedure *says*— about Ashley, and about other people with disabilities (WPAS 2007). Making such a radical change to what appears to be a medically healthy body seems to some to concede that the problem is the body, not the society that fails to accommodate it (see Chapter 13). This says something that many disabled people take to be false, and also harmful to them and their prospect for greater inclusion in society. The procedure also seems, to some, to say something about Ashley herself: that she is, somehow, less than the rest of us, that she does not deserve the same opportunities. It is, frankly, hard to evaluate these claims, though they have a ring of truth—what does it mean, anyway, for doing something to say something? Some defenders argue that if this procedure says anything, it simply says that this is what is best for Ashley, staying silent on deeper political and philosophical matters (Diekema and Fost 2010). Whether they are right or not, what is best for Ashley does in the end seem to be the central issue: her parents' primary concern is, and should be, doing what is best for her, rather than saying the best things about her or people like her.

SUGGESTED READINGS

The case of Ashley X was originally reported by the treating physicians (and with the consent of the parents), in:

Gunther, Daniel F., and Douglas S. Diekema. 2006. "Attenuating Growth in Children with Profound Developmental Disability: A New Approach to an Old Dilemma." *Archives of Pediatrics and Adolescent Medicine* 160 (10): 1013–17. https://doi.org/10.1001/archpedi.160.10.1013.

Among the initial, highly critical, responses, to the growth-attenuating procedures, were:

Gerald D. Coleman. 2007. "The Irreversible Disabling of a Child." *The National Catholic Bioethics Quarterly* 7 (4): 711–28. https://doi.org/10.5840/ncbq2007747.

Washington Protection & Advocacy System. 2007. "Investigative Report Regarding the 'Ashley Treatment.'" https://www.disabilityrightswa.org/reports/investigative-report-regarding-ashley-treatment/.

For a response from one of the original physicians, see:

Diekema, Douglas S., and Norman Fost. 2010. "Ashley Revisited: A Response to the Critics." *American Journal of Bioethics* 10 (1): 30–44. https://doi.org/10.1080/15265160903469336.

For further factual context, and supporting ethical analysis, see:

Edwards, Steven D. 2011. "The Case of Ashley X." *Clinical Ethics* 6 (1): 39–44. https://doi.org/10.1258/ce.2011.011007.

On the moral importance, or lack thereof, of biological "normality," see:

Wakefield, J. C. 1992. "The Concept of Mental Disorder: On the Boundary between Biological Facts and Social Values." *The American Psychologist* 47 (3): 373–88. https://doi.org/10.1037/0003-066X.47.3.373.

And for a recent and influential critical take on the Ashley case from a major philosopher of intellectual disability:

Kittay, Eva Feder. 2011. "The Strange Case of Ashley X." *Hypatia* 26 (3): 610–31.

16

DILEMMAS OF DECISION-MAKING

Kill Mary to Save Jodie?

THE CASE

Parents, as we have seen, often have to make wrenching decisions about their disabled children. Few decisions are more wrenching than this one:

In 1993 a woman delivered conjoined twins, Mary and Jodie, who were linked at the pelvis. Mary had a "primitive" brain, and the lungs and heart on Mary's side of the body functioned very poorly, so both twins relied for oxygenated blood on the functioning heart and organs on Jodie's side of the body. If nothing was done, the one functioning cardiovascular system would wear out in a year or two and both girls would die. However, if surgeons separated the twins now, Jodie would have a very good chance of having a normal life and lifespan. But this would require clamping off the artery keeping Mary alive, and she would die immediately. The hospital wanted to separate the twins now, but the parents opposed the operation on the grounds that the surgeons would be murdering Mary to save Jodie. The parents sought a court order to stop the hospital from operating, but ultimately the courts decided in favor of the hospital, the separation surgery was performed, Mary died immediately, and Jodie has gone on to live a normal life.

DOI: 10.4324/9781032640525-20

This case raises two very difficult questions: did the separation surgery murder or otherwise wrong Mary, and should the decision have been left to the parents? Here we will focus on the first question, but it may be kept in mind that it is possible to think the surgery would not wrong Mary and still think that the hospital and the state should not have overruled the parents' wishes.

RESPONSES

Rarely do conjoined twins wish to be separated later in life. But growing up conjoined was not an option for Mary and Jodie, and it was only if what is known as a "sacrifice surgery" were performed—where one twin is sacrificed for the sake of the other—that one of the twins, Jodie, would have a good chance of surviving long-term. Had it been possible to perform such a surgery when the twins were still fetuses, it might have been easier to justify. There may also have been fewer qualms about the surgery if, had it not been performed, Mary's remaining life would have been very brief or so awful for her that an earlier death would have been a mercy. Because Mary's brain was "primitive," it was hard to know exactly what benefits she could get out of her remaining time. But she was likely sentient and would have experienced some simple pleasures and pains and possibly some bonding with her twin and caregivers. Depriving Mary of the six months to two years she was expected to survive without separation would likely have been contrary to her interests.

On the assumptions that Mary has full moral status and an interest in continued life, it becomes difficult to see how separation can be justified. After all, we wouldn't think it was right to treat separate twins in a similar way (Dreger 2000). Imagine there was a twin that had a bad heart and a separate twin with a bad liver, and that both twins would die in six months without replacement organs. We would not think it was permissible to harvest the vital organ of one twin to save the other twin, even if the twin that is saved would gain much more than the sacrificed twin would lose. We are imagining these twins as separate of course, but why would physical conjunction make any difference to the permissibility of such a sacrifice? This is the challenge that needs to be addressed by those who wish to justify the surgery, and its defenders have tried to meet it in a variety of ways.

One defense of the sacrifice surgery is that it would not count as killing Mary but instead as merely letting her die. In Dreger's example, one twin is clearly killed to save the other, but since Mary is relying on Jodie's functioning heart and lungs for the oxygenated blood that sustains her, the thought is that surgery to separate Mary from Jodie merely withdraws aid that Jodie is providing to Mary.

Characterizing the surgery as withdrawing aid is controversial, however, since it assumes that the functioning heart and lungs on Jodie's side of the body are hers rather than the common property of the twins (Wasserman 2006). Even if those functioning organs do belong to Jodie, this may still not be enough on its own to justify the surgery. For one thing, it may not be possible to separate Mary and Jodie without violating Mary's right to bodily integrity. Moreover, even if it was possible to separate them without violating Mary's right to bodily integrity, since Mary and Jodie came into existence connected in this way (unlike you and the Violinist in Thomson's famous thought experiment, see Chapter 8), it is plausible that Mary has a right to continue using Jodie's organs (Himma 1999).

A second defense of separation is that Mary is not just using Jodie's organs but is also slowly killing Jodie (albeit innocently). Perhaps surgical separation can be justified on the grounds that the surgeons are exercising Jodie's right to self-defense on her behalf. In the graphic language of Justice Ward:

> Mary may have a right to life, but she has little right to be alive. She is alive because and only because, to put it bluntly, but nonetheless accurately, she sucks the lifeblood of Jodie and she sucks the lifeblood out of Jodie.
> (Ward and Walker 2000)

This appears to be a stronger defense than the first. Even if Mary would normally have a right to continue relying on the functioning heart and lungs, she may not have this right when this will result in Jodie's premature death. Consider the situation of Simon Yates, who was roped to Joe Simpson, his fellow mountain climber, when Simpson fell off a cliff and was suspended in the air by the rope. Yates was only able to hold Simpson up for about an hour, and with no other solution available decided to cut the rope before Simpson's weight dragged him off the mountain too and they both fell to their deaths.

The Yates–Simpson situation, however, may not be such a good analogy for the Jodie–Mary situation. For one thing, separating Simpson from Yates deprives Simpson of at most a few terror-filled minutes of life, whereas separating Mary from Jodie deprives Mary of a year or two of probably-worth-living life. For another, while it is obvious where Yates's and Simpson's bodies begin and end, this is not true of Mary and Jodie, who came into existence conjoined. If the functioning heart and lungs on Jodie's side of the body belong to both Mary and Jodie, then it would be more appropriate to describe their predicament as one in which Mary and Jodie are both housed in a body insufficient to support them long-term than as one in which Mary is threatening Jodie's life by "sucking the lifeblood out of Jodie." The situation may in fact be more analogous to one in which two people find themselves on a raft that they jointly own and that can only support the weight of one (Wasserman 2006).

A third defense of the separation appeals to the doctrine of double effect, according to which agency that results in harm to someone is harder to justify if the harm is intended than if it is merely foreseen (see Chapters 1 and 23). This defense then claims that the surgeons would not be intending Mary's death in performing the surgery that results in her death.

Strictly speaking, the physicians do not *need* Mary to die. If by some miracle Mary were to survive the cutting off her supply of oxygenated blood (perhaps her nonfunctioning organs start working), this would not prevent the surgeons from achieving their goal of saving Jodie. Still, to save Jodie they do need to produce an effect on Mary that they foresee will lead to Mary's death; namely, cutting her off from Jodie's organs, and on one influential account of the doctrine intending such an effect is still very hard to justify (Quinn 1989).

However, even if many would regard the surgeons as having problematic intentions in performing the surgery, it is also common to draw a distinction between plans that *use* the victim to achieve a goal and plans that view the victim only as an obstacle or a difficulty to be removed (Quinn 1989). Thus, even if the harm the surgeons cause Mary is harder to justify than it would have been had the surgeons not intended to have a fatal effect on Mary, it may not be as hard to justify as it would have been had Mary presented them with an opportunity to save Jodie as a potential organ donor rather than posing an obstacle to Jodie's survival.

SUGGESTED READINGS

For an early article opposing the separation:

Dreger, Alice. 2000. "Why Change the Rules for Twins Like Them?" *Washington Post*, September 24.

A careful examination of the rights that conjoined twins might have against each other:

Wasserman, David. 2006. "Conjunction and Separation: Viable Pairings, Equitable Relationships." In David Benatar (ed.), *Cutting to the Core: Exploring the Ethics of Contested Surgeries* (pp. 127–40). Lanham, MD: Rowman & Littlefield.

Uses hypothetical examples of conjoined twins to challenge the conclusions about abortion that Thomson draws from her Violinist example:

Himma, Kenneth. 1999. "Thomson's Violinist and Conjoined Twins." *Cambridge Quarterly of Healthcare Ethics* 8 (4): 428–35.

A court decision that considers a wide range of arguments for and against separating Mary and Jodie, including the Yates–Simpson analogy:

Ward, Brooke and Robert Walker. 2000. "In Re A (Children) (Conjoined Twins: Surgical Separation)," Court of Appeal.

And a seminal article on the doctrine of double effect:

Quinn, Warren S. 1989. "Actions, Intentions, and Consequences: The Doctrine of Double Effect." *Philosophy & Public Affairs* 18 (4): 334–51.

DECIDING FOR THE FUTURE
Margo's Advance Directive

THE CASE

Normally we defer to a person's current wishes rather than their earlier ones when they conflict. People are allowed to change their minds. But certain radical changes, such as the changes brought on by dementia, call this practice into question. To see how, consider the case of Margo:

When he was a medical student Andrew Firlik befriended a 55-year-old woman with Alzheimer's disease named "Margo." Margo was losing her ability to recall people and events from her past and had lost her ability to form new memories. But she was unbothered by these impairments and enjoyed a variety of simple activities, such as reading mystery novels (though her place in them jumped around), putting on makeup (thinking she was getting ready for work), making art (though she painted the same picture the same way every day), listening to music (the same song over and over), and peanut butter and jelly sandwiches. Margo was happy. In fact, Firlik says, "Despite her illness, or maybe somehow because of it, Margo is undeniably one of the happiest people I have known" (Firlik 1991).

Now suppose that before her cognitive decline Margo had authored an advance directive stating that when her dementia had progressed

DOI: 10.4324/9781032640525-21

to this stage she should not be given life-prolonging treatment, even if she was happy. Perhaps she believed that the longer she survived in such a state the more it would mar a life otherwise marked by a high degree of independence and intellectual achievement, or perhaps she wanted to bequeath a substantial sum to her children or to a charity and the costs of her care would deplete her assets. Margo now develops pneumonia that if untreated will end her life swiftly and painlessly. Should physicians respect the wishes that Margo expressed in her advance directive and withhold treatment? If Margo were miserable or in a persistent vegetative state, there would be no conflict between her earlier wishes and her current ones. But her current wish is to live, or at least to continue engaging in those activities she enjoys, and she no longer cares about the things that prompted those earlier wishes, like her dignity or the costs of her care.

RESPONSES

The standard view in medical ethics is that respect for Margo's autonomy requires honoring her advance directive, so long as she was competent when she wrote it, was adequately informed and unpressured, and did not subsequently change her mind while still competent.

One objection to the standard view is that by the later stages of dementia memory loss is so profound that the individual to whom the directive would be applied is not the same individual as its author. Since autonomy rights are rights to control what is done to oneself, respecting Margo's autonomy could not demand that we give her control over someone else's fate.

One way to defend the standard view against this objection is to challenge the claim that the author of the advance directive and the patient are numerically distinct individuals. Biological accounts of identity over time only require biological continuity, and whatever their psychological differences, Late Margo is the same human animal as Early Margo (DeGrazia 1999). Even according to most psychological accounts of identity, there need not be a chain of memories linking Later Margo to Early Margo for them to be identical. Identity is not just about memory and so long as Later Margo has inherited enough other aspects of Early Margo's psychology, she would remain the same individual (Holton 2016).

Even if Early and Later Margo are identical, however, it remains puzzling why respect for autonomy would require honoring the advance directive, as the standard view insists. Normally when someone's wishes have changed, we take respect for autonomy to require deference to their current wishes, even if we think their previous wishes were better or formed under more favorable circumstances. Why not disregard Margo's previous wishes and respect her current ones instead?

Ronald Dworkin defends the standard view against this challenge. Dworkin acknowledges that normally we respect someone's autonomy by deferring to someone's current rather than their previous wishes even when their current wishes are weak-willed. For example, we would be required to administer a blood transfusion to a Jehovah's Witness patient who, having lost their nerve on the verge of surgery, had a change of mind. But now suppose that when this patient requests the transfusion they are not merely weak-willed but temporarily deranged. Here we are inclined to think that respect for the deranged patient's autonomy, unlike the weak-willed patient's, would require honoring their earlier wishes and denying them the transfusion. Dworkin concludes that it is only if the change of mind constitutes a "fresh exercise of autonomy" that respect for autonomy demands respecting the later wishes. Thus, if Margo, like the deranged Jehovah's Witness patient, is incapable of a fresh exercise of autonomy, then respecting her autonomy would require honoring her advance directive, despite her conflicting current wishes.

But what is this special capacity for autonomy whose free exercise is so important that we should not interfere even to prevent people from making serious and even fatal mistakes? According to Dworkin's "integrity account" of this capacity, it is the capacity to lead a life whose structure reflects our deepest values or sense of self, giving the narrative of our life an overall integrity. Early Margo was exercising this capacity when she wrote the advance directive. By contrast, Later Margo's memory impairments render her unable to think about her life as a whole and thus unable to even consider the question of what sort of final chapter to her life would cohere best with the preceding narrative. Even if Margo had retained this ability to set standards for her life, her cognitive deficits would make her unable to *implement* those standards, i.e., to select the appropriate means to her ends. Since,

18

MY DECISION ALONE?

Family, Community, and Consent in Global Context

THE CASE

According to the currently prevailing model of consent in medicine in much of the West, if a patient is a competent adult and conscious, then it is morally necessary to obtain their consent before treating them. This model, which we can call the "autonomy model," also regards an adult patient's consent as sufficient in the sense that no one else's consent is needed to make treatment permissible.

The autonomy model, a relatively recent development in the West, has not been embraced in many regions of the world (see also Chapter 3). In some rural patriarchal communities in sub-Saharan Africa, for example, a male authority must consent on behalf of adult women. This can present physicians who accept this model but practice medicine in a community that rejects it with a dilemma.

To illustrate, suppose that a pregnant adult woman arrives alone at a free clinic in labor. It is soon apparent that her pregnancy is obstructed and that she will die without an emergency C-section. According to the norms in this community, blood transfusions and surgeries can only be performed with the consent of the woman's father (Gogenini 2012). She asks the physician to contact her father to get his permission to operate. Unable to reach her father, the physician returns and

DOI: 10.4324/9781032640525-22

tells her that any further delay could cost her life. Reluctantly, she tells the physician to go ahead with the surgery.

Since the local norms insist on the father's actual consent and make no exception for emergencies, administering the C-section in this situation would be a clear violation of those norms. The physician, who works for a non-governmental organization (NGO), disagrees with those norms but worries that violating them could anger the community and mean the end of the clinic, which is the only source of healthcare for many women in this community. Should the physician comply with those norms and refuse to treat her?

RESPONSES

In a traditional community like this one it would be rare for an adult woman to want treatment when the wishes of a male authority are either unknown or are opposed to treatment. Normally the woman, who has been socialized to defer to the wishes of a male authority, would align her preferences with his. Even here ethical concerns can arise.

There may be grounds for doubting the autonomy of consent that is governed in this way by someone else's decision. Normally when a patient prefers that someone else, such as a family member or the physician, make a treatment decision, it is because they wish to relieve themselves of the burden of making the decision. But we are imagining that the adult woman prefers that her father make the decision, not because she doesn't feel up to the task, but because she believes it is her *duty* to defer to the wishes of the male authority. Some ethicists would argue that, insofar as her conception of those duties is a product of oppressive socialization, decisions she makes on that basis are not autonomous (Stoljar 2018).

A distinct concern that arises when a woman aligns her preferences with those of a male authority is that her preferences might be a product of coercion. That is, she might prefer what he prefers, not out of a sense of duty, but out of fear of the consequences of defying his will. It is typically assumed that whenever consent is coerced, it is non-autonomous and invalid. But there is a difference of opinion in the literature about consent that is coerced, not by the agent who is receiving the consent but a third party. Some ethicists have argued that only coercion by the party receiving the consent can invalidate it (for discussions see Millum 2013 and Gerver 2021). If this view is correct, then unless the doctor could and should do something to make the male authority withdraw his threat or prevent him from carrying it out, it may be acceptable to treat the woman with her consent even though her consent is a product of coercion. The implications of the autonomy model, then, are far from clear when a woman consents to treatment only because a male authority wants her to have it. Its implications are much clearer in those cases, like the one above, where the woman consents and the male authority cannot be reached or refuses to give permission; namely, her consent suffices. Thus, a physician practicing in a community like this one where the norms require male consent will be forced to choose between adherence to the autonomy model and adherence to the local norms, at least on some occasions.

One way out of the dilemma would be to give up the autonomy model or qualify it. Ethicists have argued in favor of alternative models that permit a competent patient's *family* to have the final say under certain conditions (Hardwig 1990). But these alternative models treat men and women symmetrically, and under the local norms in this community it is only women who need male consent, not vice versa.

What should the physician do? One option would be to ignore the local norms. This would mean performing the emergency C-section with the woman's consent, even when her father refuses or cannot be reached. But if the community takes these norms very seriously, violating these norms could cost the physician the opportunity to continue practicing in this community and deprive women of essential healthcare.

Another option would be to follow the local norms. This would mean refraining from performing the emergency C-section when the father opposes it or is unreachable, even when the woman consents. The advantage of this option is that it protects the opportunity to serve this community. The disadvantages are that it fails to fully respect the woman's rights and legitimizes norms that subordinate women to men. Physicians might find it tolerable to refrain from treating a consenting woman when the local norms forbid it, since the local norms could be viewed as just another constraint on the physician's powers to aid, on a par with lacking state-of-the-art facilities, equipment, and medicine. But if a woman ever refused to consent to a treatment that the male authority wanted her to have, the local norms would require treating her against her will, and that's a line most physicians would be unwilling to cross.

A third option would be to adopt a compromise approach that cooperates enough with the local norms to maintain a good relationship with the community but also tries to avoid or blunt the worst consequences of those norms. Such an approach might adopt some of the strategies that were used by an NGO-sponsored clinic in a community with the local norms described.

This NGO decided that the only way it could continue serving this community was if its physicians complied with the local norm of not treating adult women without the consent of a male authority. There was just no way around it. Since this norm requires the father's actual consent even in emergencies, it forbids performing a life-saving C-section not only when the father opposes the surgery but also when the father simply cannot be reached in time. The NGO's solution to situations where the father cannot be reached was to ask fathers of pregnant women to fill out advance directives specifying which emergency procedures they consent to in the event they cannot be reached.

SUGGESTED READINGS

For a description of Somali cultural norms regarding healthcare, where a woman's husband's or father's consent is required for all healthcare decisions:

   Gogenini, Roopa. January 5, 2012. "In Mogadishu, Nothing Is Simple." United Nations Population Fund.

For a comprehensive look at competing accounts of relational autonomy and their motivations:

   Stoljar, Natalie. 2018. "Feminist Perspectives on Autonomy." *Stanford Encyclopedia of Philosophy*. In https://plato.stanford.edu/entries/feminism-autonomy/.

For analyses of consent that has been coerced by someone other than the receiver of that consent:

   Millum, Joseph. 2013. "Consent Under Pressure: The Puzzle of Third-Party Coercion." *Ethical Theory and Moral Practice* 17 (1): 113–27.

   Gerver, Mollie. 2021. "Consent and Third-Party Coercion." *Ethics* 131 (2): 246–69.

For a model of medical decision-making that gives the family the final say over the objections of a competent adult patient in certain situations:

Hardwig, John. 1990. "What About the Family?" *The Hastings Center Report* 20 (2): 5–10.

For a discussion of a related dilemma for women in oppressive cultures—either play it safe through subordination to the oppressive local norms or oppose those norms at one's own risk—see:

Khader, Serene J. 2020. "The Feminist Case Against Relational Autonomy." *Journal of Moral Philosophy* 17 (5): 499–526.

For an argument against the Saudi Arabian requirement of a husband's consent for an elective hysterectomy:

Muaygil, Ruaim. "Her Uterus, Her Medical Decision? Dismantling Spousal Consent for Medically Indicated Hysterectomies in Saudi Arabia." *Cambridge Quarterly of Healthcare Ethics* 27 (3): 397–407.

PART V

DECIDING FOR YOURSELF

19

WRONGS WITHOUT HARMS?

Two Cases on the Basis of Informed Consent

THE CASES

It's natural to think that, in bioethics and ethics more generally, the main thing, maybe the only thing, is to avoid unjustifiably *harming* others, or making them worse off. This can seem, even, to underlie *autonomy* or self-rule as the central principle of bioethics: one central reason why we shouldn't do things to people's bodies, without their consent, is that people tend to feel profoundly violated when others touch or make use of their bodies without their consent.

No one would deny that this is *one reason* why it is important to get consent before touching someone else's body, in a medical context or otherwise. But philosophers and bioethicists have questioned whether this harm, and harm more broadly, is the *only* reason why it is important that we respect people's wishes about their own body. Some philosophers suggest that there is such a thing as *harmless wrongdoing*; that, sometimes, it is wrong to touch or use somebody's body without their consent even though they are not harmed in any way.

Some possible examples come from the real world. In American medical schools, up until very recently, it was a common practice to train students in human anatomy by allowing them to conduct clinical exams on patients who were anesthetized for purposes of

DOI: 10.4324/9781032640525-24

gynecological surgery (Friesen 2018). In many cases, patients were not informed that their bodies would be used for this educational purpose, or asked whether they would consent to it. Generally, however, the exams posed little to no physical risk to the patient. And because they were entirely unconscious throughout, and were generally not told of the exams before or after, there seems to be little chance of psychological trauma.

This real-world example, like real-world examples generally, raises many messy issues. Patients may have been at some risk of physical harm from clumsy students even in cases where no actual damage occurred. Similarly, in the real world there is always some risk that the patient would find out and feel violated, as a result of incomplete anesthesia or reading about the practice later in newspapers or bioethics textbooks.

The philosopher David Archard (2008) has devised a simpler example, which makes the same basic point while abstracting away from these complexities. In Archard's example someone simply inserts a cotton swab into your mouth, while you are unconscious, and without specific permission, to collect a sample for research purposes. This still seems wrong even though there really is no appreciable risk of physical harm here, and even if we assume you have just about zero chance of being psychologically harmed by finding out.

DISCUSSION

Do these examples show that there can be such a thing as harmless wrongdoing (Ripstein 2006)? Many might be inclined to resist this, thinking that what makes bodily invasions wrong is the distinctive sorts of harms they produce. After all, normally when we think about morality we think about harm: usually, if I have an objection to your treatment of me, it is because you have injured me or made me worse off in some way.

Some might simply insist that, because these actions are harmless, nothing has gone wrong here. This is hard to believe: the cases, the exams in particular, shock the conscience. A more plausible approach would be to say that, in some of these cases at least, there is a sort of consent after all, *tacit* or *presumed* consent (for critical discussion see Friesen 2018). Tacit consent—where one agrees to something by not objecting to it—seems like a bad model here, since neither Archard's patient nor unconscious subjects of exam are aware that there is anything to object to. *Presumed* consent, the idea that we can proceed as if consent would be present when we are confident the patient *would* consent, also looks like a bad fit for these cases. Presumed consent arguments seem most forceful where proceeding without actual consent would be obviously beneficial, as in emergency surgery on unconscious patients. But in the case of the swab, or the gynecological exams, what is the reason not to get consent in the first place? It is hard to see how this benefits the patient; thus, hard to see why we should assume they would be fine with our proceeding without asking them.

If, for these reasons, we think the exams, and swabs, are wrongful after all, we will need to decide whether they are wrong because they are harmful or for some other reason. Proponents of the idea that wrongs are always harmful could say various things here. One would be that the patient is harmed because their *autonomy* or control of their lives is set back. (Dworkin 1988). This may be so in some cases—the pelvic exams—but probably not in others. As Archard points out, a minor non-consenting touch, like a mouth swab, does not change the story of my life as a whole, and thus does not reduce my control over it. The difference between the two cases suggests that autonomy harms, if understood in this way, could not be a complete explanation: we need to know what aspects of my life I *ought* to control, to know when I have a setback in my autonomy. The same can likely be said for attempted explanations that point to my simply preferring that this not happen. I might prefer that my readers be fascinated with my book, but that does not mean they wrong me if they are a bit bored.

Similar concerns arise for the proposal that the swab, or the exams, are wrong, because they are *indignities* (Foster 2014). This seems clear in the case of the swab, and even more clear in the exams, where the involvement of "private parts" puts dignity especially at stake. But again, we seem to require an explanation for *why* our dignity is bound up in controlling what happens to our bodies—not least, to understand why there are more or worse dignity harms in genital examination than in unconsenting touch of the mouth or nose.

Cases like the swab, and the exam, then, suggest that there is more to right and wrong in bioethics than harms to the person wronged. What else? We can imagine various proposals to account for these cases.

Friesen, in discussing gynecological exams, considers risks to the physician–patient relationship and the medical system more broadly. If people can't trust their physicians to ask them before doing things like this, they may be less likely to agree to undergo procedures that involve anesthesia, or to visit physicians at all. More generally, bad publicity in cases like this may undermine trust in medical authorities, particularly among groups who already have reason to distrust that system (see Bird 2007). That can be harmful to both individual and public health, if members of the public, or particular groups, refuse to take valid medical advice (about vaccines, say) as a result (see for instance Chapters 29, 34, 37). The idea is that these actions are wrong because rules permitting them are harmful *to society*. This explanation may be harder to extend to the swab, though. Allowing trivial, pointless physical touching like this does not pose much of a threat to patients: because it is trivial, there's little reason to fear it; because it is pointless, there's little reason to worry that it will happen even if allowed.

It is no simple matter, then, to account for what has gone wrong in the case of the exams, or the swabs. But it is hard to dispel the strong feeling that something has. Perhaps there is not much more to say here than that each of us has a basic, though perhaps not absolute, right to decide what happens to our bodies (Thomson 1990). What goes wrong, in both of these cases, then, is simply that a doctor makes a decision that is really a patient's to make.

SUGGESTED READINGS

For discussion of non-consensual gynecological exams, and a detailed rebuttal of several possible defenses of the practice, see:

Friesen, Phoebe. 2018. "Educational Pelvic Exams on Anesthetized Women: Why Consent Matters." *Bioethics* 32 (5): 298–307. https://doi.org/10.1111/bioe.12441.

For the swab case, as an argument that our bodily rights are not based in harm, autonomy, or self-ownership, see:

Archard, David. 2008. "Informed Consent: Autonomy and Self-Ownership." *Journal of Applied Philosophy* 25 (1): 19–34. https://www.jstor.org/stable/24354973

For the general issue of harmless wrongdoing, and the relation of harming to wronging more generally, see:

Ripstein, Arthur. 2006. "Beyond the Harm Principle." *Philosophy & Public Affairs* 34 (3): 215–45. https://www.jstor.org/stable/3876391

Bird, Colin. 2007. "Harm Versus Sovereignty: A Reply to Ripstein." *Philosophy & Public Affairs* 35 (2): 179–94. https://www.jstor.org/stable/4623787

On the idea that consent violations are harms to autonomy:

Dworkin, Gerald. 1988. "Autonomy and Informed Consent." In *The Theory and Practice of Autonomy* (pp. 100–20). New York: Cambridge University Press. http://dx.doi.org/10.1017/CBO9780511625206.008.

On the idea that they are primarily harms to dignity:

Foster, Charles. 2014. "Dignity and the Use of Body Parts." *Journal of Medical Ethics* 40 (1): 44–7. https://doi.org/10.1136/medethics-2012-100763.

Finally, for a perspicuous statement and extended defense of the idea that rights in the body are a special category, independent of harm, see:

Thomson, Judith Jarvis. 1990. *The Realm of Rights*. Cambridge, MA: Harvard University Press.

WHO IS COMPETENT TO CONSENT?

Anorexia Nervosa

THE CASE

When patients make decisions that seem extremely unreasonable, their caregivers must determine whether they made that decision because they lack capacity or merely because they have unusual values. If it's the latter, there is a consensus in medical ethics that it must be respected, even if that decision is fatal. Disorders like anorexia nervosa might challenge that consensus.

Elizabeth is a 20-year-old female who has severe anorexia nervosa (AN), a disorder characterized by low weight, fear of gaining weight, and a distorted perception of body size. Her body mass index (BMI) is dangerously low. If she gains weight her clinical team thinks she could eventually make a full recovery, but if she does not take in calories, her death is imminent. The clinical team explains the situation to Elizabeth, but she still refuses food. To prevent Elizabeth from making what her clinicians and family regard as a tragic mistake, they consider feeding her against her will using physical or chemical restraints. Although clinicians normally respect refusals of even life-saving treatment, they believe the fact that Elizabeth's refusal is caused by her eating disorder justifies overriding her wishes in this instance.

May the clinicians override Elizabeth's refusal?

DOI: 10.4324/9781032640525-25

RESPONSES

When paternalism reigned in medicine, clinicians would override a patient's refusal of care when they judged the refusal to be contrary to the patient's best interests. The current approach emphasizes respect for the patient's autonomy. Respect for autonomy, in turn, is usually operationalized as respecting a patient's refusal of treatment when, but only when, the patient has sufficient capacity to make the treatment decision for themselves.

Having sufficient decision-making capacity (DMC) to make a particular treatment decision is typically understood as requiring possession of the following abilities to a sufficient degree (Appelbaum 2007):

(a)   the ability to *make and express a decision* about that treatment;
(b   the ability to *value* or at least to form relatively stable preferences;
(c)   the ability to *understand* what the physicians are trying to communicate about the treatment;
(d)   the ability to *appreciate* this information, which requires the ability to believe, not merely understand, what is being communicated and to apply the information to oneself; and
(e)   the ability to *reason*, which includes abilities to draw inferences about the likely consequences of various options, to weigh up the pros and cons of each option in light of one's values, and to compare the options to arrive at judgment of what it would be best to do.

Since Elizabeth has made and expressed a decision to refuse treatment and since her preferences are stable, assessment of her DMC would focus on her possession of abilities (c)–(e).

Having a low BMI can interfere with one's ability to pay attention and to process information, which could compromise abilities (c) to understand and (e) to reason. As one patient reported: "once you've lost a lot of weight, your thought processes are all muddled" and "your brain doesn't work very well" (Tan et al. 2006).

Even if Elizabeth is alert and able to understand and process what the clinicians are saying, AN might still compromise (d), her ability to appreciate her situation. Patients suffering from AN misperceive their body size, which sometimes (though not always) leads them to form false beliefs about their situation, such as "I am not dangerously thin." For example, one patient, in response to being asked whether death could result from her refusal to eat, said: "Not to me . . . Because you have to be really thin to die, and I'm fat, so it won't happen to me" (Tan et al. 2006).

When abilities (c)–(e) are compromised, this will impair a patient's ability to reach a judgment about accepting or refusing food that reflects her values. For example, even if a patient values her health more than being thin, she will have difficulty reaching the judgment that it would be better to accept food if her false beliefs about her situation (e.g., that she is fat) prevent her from recognizing that refusing to eat is jeopardizing her health.

But AN does not always compromise these abilities. Indeed, there are AN patients who fully grasp the implications of continuing to refuse food and still refuse it. Why? Sometimes it is because, although they value their health more than thinness and recognize that they should eat, their *volitional* ability to make and stick to a decision that reflects that judgment is overwhelmed by their compulsion to refuse food (Gert et al. 1997). In the same way some patients with a phobia of needles cannot bring themselves to consent to an injection they know they need, sometimes AN patients who sincerely judge it better to eat still reject the food, to their frustration. As one patient reported:

> I'd be thinking, "oh I really want to eat . . ." And when it came to it, my hands would start shaking and I'd just want to throw it across the room, I just couldn't do it, no matter how hard tried I just couldn't physically do it."
>
> (Hope et al. 2013)

When patients' cognitive abilities to reach a judgment that reflects their values or their volitional abilities to make and maintain a decision that reflects their judgment are deeply compromised, it is easy to defend a choice to override their refusal on the grounds that their refusal is non-autonomous. But there are also AN patients who refuse food who have none of these deficits. As surprising as it may seem, they refuse food, not because they have trouble making a decision that reflects their values, but because they have unusual values. They may not have started out this way, but over time they have come to identify with their AN and to view their anorexia-rooted desires as correct and authentic.

> It's awful to admit, but in general it's the most important thing in my life . . . And even now if I were given the opportunity to go back now [to university] but I'd have to be a lot heavier, I'd say no.
>
> (Tan et al. 2006)

If Elizabeth were refusing food only because she valued thinness more than anything else, must her refusal be respected? Many ethicists are inclined to say no. But they have had difficulty explaining why.

Elizabeth's refusal is certainly contrary to her best interests. But it is a widely shared assumption that the correctness of a patient's values is irrelevant to the question of whether a refusal based on those values is autonomous. This assumption, indeed, is embedded in the concept of DMC, which is why possession of DMC is based on an assessment of a patient's abilities to translate their values into action rather than on the content of those values.

One ethicist has argued that we must reject the assumption that a decision can count as autonomous and yet be seriously mistaken (Kious 2015). This proposal would license Elizabeth's caregivers to save her life, but it comes at a steep price, since it amounts to the rejection of a foundational assumption of medical ethics for over 50 years; namely, that concern for autonomy sometimes requires us to let people make their own mistakes, even deadly mistakes.

A less radical solution would identify a reason for regarding Elizabeth's values as non-autonomous that is independent of their being mistaken. One possibility is that her values are a product of pathology (Tan 2006). The extreme importance she places on thinness is a symptom of her illness. This option allows us to explain why concern for autonomy would not require respecting Elizabeth's refusal and perhaps suicidal refusals of food by severely clinical depressed patients but would still require respecting refusals of food from politically motivated hunger strikers, even though we might regard their decisions as equally unwise.

Some, however, have argued that there is no way to explain why the pathological origin of Elizabeth's values would render them non-autonomous without invoking the idea that her values are mistaken

(Kious 2015). If that is correct, then the claim that her decision is non-autonomous because her values have a pathological origin is just disguised paternalism.

Another possible solution claims that the value placed on thinness by people with AN probably does not reflect their deepest selves – that at some level, they do not really have the distorted values in question, but only think they do. The evidence for this is that even patients who espouse this value also tend to have mixed feelings about it at the time and when they have later recovered and look back, they often feel regret about having prioritized thinness over relationships, education, and everything else (Craigie 2009). Whether this solution is ultimately persuasive or not, it does appear to avoid paternalism, since evidence of this sort is not meant to show that their values are objectively mistaken but only that the value is not truly authentic.

SUGGESTED READINGS

For two compelling challenges to the common view that respect for autonomy requires respect for all and only those decisions made by patients with decision-making capacity:

> Martin, Adrienne. 2007. "Tales Publicly Allowed: Competence, Capacity, and Religious Belief." *Hastings Center Report* 37 (1): 33–40.

> Schwan, Ben. 2021. "Why Decision-Making Capacity Matters." *Journal of Moral Philosophy* 19(5): 447–73.

A succinct statement of the most popular competence assessment measure in medicine:

> Appelbaum, Paul. 2007. "Assessment of Patients' Competence to Consent to Treatment." *New England Journal of Medicine* 357 (18): 1834–40.

Fascinating excerpts from extensive interviews with AN patients, along with analysis:

> Tan, Jacinta, Tony Hope, Anne Stewart, and Raymond Fitzpatrick. 2006. "Competence to Make Treatment Decisions in Anorexia Nervosa: Thinking Processes and Values." *Philosophy, Psychiatry, & Psychology* 13 (4): 267–82.

> Hope, Tony, Jacinta Tan, Anne Stewart, and Ray Fitzpatrick. 2011. "Anorexia Nervosa and the Language of Authenticity." *Hastings Center Report* 41 (6): 19–29.

> Hope, Tony, Jacinta Tan, Anne Stewart, and John McMillan. 2013. "Agency, Ambivalence and Authenticity: The Many Ways in Which Anorexia Nervosa Can Affect Autonomy." *International Journal of Law in Context* 9 (1): 20–36.

Argues that traditional competence assessments neglect deficits in volitional abilities:

> Gert, Bernard, Charles Culver, and K. Danner Clouser. 1997. "Chapter 6: Competence." in *Bioethics: A Return to Fundamentals* (pp. 133–5). Oxford: Oxford University Press.

Argues that we cannot justify overriding AN patients' refusals without giving up value-neutrality:

> Kious, Brent. 2015. "Autonomy and Values: Why the Conventional Theory of Autonomy is not Value-Neutral." *Philosophy, Psychiatry, & Psychology* 22 (1): 1–12.

Presents a novel autonomy-based justification for involuntary treatment of patients with AN:

> Craigie, Jillian. 2009. "Competence, Practical Rationality and What a Patient Values." *Bioethics* 25 (6): 326–33.

THE ETHICS OF INFLUENCE, I
A Clinical Nudge

THE CASE

Our decisions are often subject to seemingly non-rational influences. Instead of lamenting this fact, perhaps we should recruit these influences to help patients make better decisions for themselves. Consider the following case:

Dr. Reyes, a fictional physician, has been helping her patients avoid unwanted treatments by presenting them with an advance directive that spells out different end-of-life care options. She is confident that these advance directives have reduced the number of her patients who receive unwanted life-extending care, which is a serious problem in the United States. She then comes across a study that suggests that she could reduce that number even further by making some small adjustments to the forms. In this study patients were randomly selected to receive one of three different advance directive forms (Halpern 2020). The standard form invited patients to check either of two boxes, one to request life-extending therapy (e.g., CPR, ventilation, dialysis, or feeding tubes) if needed and the other to request comfort care only. Another form made comfort care the default by having the box next to it already checked and instructing the patient that if they prefer life extension, they need to cross out the line about comfort care

DOI: 10.4324/9781032640525-26

and write their initials next to the life-extending care option. The third form made life-extending care the default in the same way. These adjustments to the forms had a surprisingly large influence on patients' choices: 61 percent of patients receiving the standard form chose comfort care; 77 percent of patients who received the form with comfort care as the default stuck with that option; only 43 percent of patients who received the form with life-extending care as the default overrode that default and chose comfort care instead.

Should Dr. Reyes replace her standard form with one that makes comfort care the default option? She wants to minimize the risk of her patients receiving unwanted treatment, but she is also uncomfortable with influencing her patients' choices in this way.

RESPONSES

Even when patients are well-informed, they are, like all of us, imperfect at translating their values into action. Having the information does not guarantee they will use it when deliberating. Even when they deliberate well and reach a judgment about what to do that reflects their values, they can still fail to make a decision that reflects that judgment through a failure to exercise enough self-control.

What can be done to improve their decision-making? One possibility is to change the patient by eliminating their irrational tendencies. Another is to change the patient's options by removing the bad option or by making the bad option more costly. But we could also leave the patient and their options as they are and strategically alter the way those options are presented to the patient. This is called "nudging" (Thaler and Sunstein 2021). Making comfort care the default option is one example. Proponents of nudges do not recommend using them to impose one's own values on the patient, which would be too paternalistic, but only to steer them in a direction that aligns with the patient's own values. So long as Dr. Reyes's aim is restricted to helping her patients better realize their own values, what objection could there be to her use of a nudge?

One concern is that some patients who prefer life-extending care will nevertheless stick with comfort care when it is the default. However, in the study mentioned above, 23 percent of the patients who received the form with the comfort care default crossed it out and initialed the option of life-extending care instead, and none of the patients who stuck with the comfort care default changed their mind in favor of the life-extending option after being debriefed and given an opportunity to revise their choice. This indicates that the nudge's influence was not overpowering.

Another concern is that this form of influence is (wrongfully) manipulative (Blumenthal-Barby 2021). Whether this objection is sound will depend both on what makes an influence manipulative and the way defaults influence decisions. According to one account of manipulation, an influence is manipulative when it induces faulty mental states or faulty transitions between mental states (Noggle 2017). Deception is manipulative in this sense because it induces false beliefs. So is inducing inappropriate emotions and making a trivial or irrelevant factor salient, since this attracts attention to the factor that exceeds the factor's importance.

Defaults can influence decisions in different ways (Beraldo and Karpus 2021). Sometimes people tend to choose the default because they are deterred by the costs of actively making another choice. If the added costs do the work, then this form of influence does not depend for its success on inducing any faulty mental states. In the present case the effort of switching would appear to be too low to explain the influence of the default, since the patient only needs to cross out a line and write their initials in front of another option. However, it is still possible that the patient is deterred from deliberating about over-riding the default by the unpleasantness of contemplating their death. Another possibility is that the default influences patients because it communicates to the patient that the physician or the medical community recommends this option. Recommendations can influence deliberations without inducing any faulty mental states, and so would not by this standard be manipulative. Finally, the default may rely on loss aversion for its influence. As the default, comfort care becomes the reference point, and from this reference point life-extending care will be viewed as offering a gain in life but a loss in comfort. Insofar as this mechanism relies on our tendency to give too much weight to facts framed as losses in our deliberations, this mechanism could count as manipulative.

Dr. Reyes's justification for making comfort care the default is to steer patients towards the option that aligns with their own values. But

the values of patients might be incomplete. They might prefer comfort care in one respect and life-extending care in another but have
no all-things-considered preference between them because they have
never decided whether they prize comfort or life extension more.
It would not be surprising if most patients lacked such a preference,
since it may be their first time seriously contemplating a tradeoff
between comfort and life.

Some ethicists argue that although the usual justification for nudges
is unavailable in such cases, a different justification is available (Gorin
et al. 2017). They claim that there is no such thing as a neutral presentation of options. We may not be able to predict how a presentation
will influence a decision, but it will. So, if a patient has no preference
between comfort and life-extending care, and Dr. Reyes believes that
comfort care is more likely to be in her best interests, then why not
nudge that patient towards comfort care? The alternative to nudging is not for Dr. Reyes to present the options in a way that avoids
having an arbitrary influence on the patient's decision, but to take
a chance that the way she presents the options (say, by using the
standard form) would arbitrarily influence that patient in the direction of life-extending care. That would be irresponsible, they argue.
One potential downside is that nudging these patients rather than
encouraging them to decide whether they value comfort or longevity
more would deprive them of an opportunity to exercise a valuable
kind of "formative" autonomy (Raskoff 2022).

SUGGESTED READINGS

This is just one of many studies conducted by the head of the UK's "Nudge
Unit":
  Halpern, S. D., D. S. Small, and A. B. Troxel. 2020. "Effect of Default Options
  in Advance Directives on Hospital-Free Days and Care Choices Among
  Seriously Ill Patients." *JAMA Network Open* 3 (3): e201742.
The classic definition and defense of nudging:
  Thaler, Richard, and Cass Sunstein. 2021. *Nudge: The Final Edition*. Revised.
  New York: Penguin Books.
A comprehensive source for both ethical assessments of nudges of various kinds
and empirical studies on human decision-making:
  Blumenthal-Barby, Jennifer. 2021. *Good Ethics and Bad Choices: The Relevance
  of Behavioral Economics for Medical Ethics*. Amsterdam: Amsterdam University
  Press.

For a useful account of manipulation and its application to nudges that raise the salience of certain facts:

Noggle, Robert. 2017. "Manipulation, Salience, and Nudges." *Bioethics* 32 (3): 164–70.

For a discussion of different possible mechanisms for the influence of defaults on decision-making:

Beraldo, Sergio, and Jurgis Karpus. 2021. "Nudging to Donate Organs: Do What You like or like What We Do?" *Medicine, Health Care and Philosophy* 24 (3): 329–40.

A novel defense of nudging in the direction of best interests when patients' preferences are incomplete:

Gorin, Moti, Steven Joffe, Neal Dickert, and Scott Halpern. 2017. "Justifying Clinical Nudges." *Hastings Center Report* 47 (2): 32–38.

For the objection to Gorin et al.'s defense, see:

Raskoff, Sarah Zoe. 2022. "Nudges and Hard Choices." *Bioethics* 36 (9): 948–56.

22

THE ETHICS OF INFLUENCE, II
The Nocebo Effect

THE CASE

We cannot decide for ourselves without information about the medical decision we are making. As the following case illustrates, though, that information can sometimes do harm as well as good.

A patient presents to the clinic with an enlarged prostate gland that is causing painful urination. The doctor wants to recommend the drug Finasteride, which is usually effective in shrinking the gland but also has side effects, including sexual dysfunction. Since the patient would probably want to take the possibility of this side effect into consideration when deciding whether to accept this treatment, the doctor initially plans to disclose this information to the patient. But then the doctor comes across a study (Mondaini et al. 2007) that gives them pause. The researchers found that when the possibility of sexual dysfunction was not disclosed, only 15 percent of patients experienced it, but when it was disclosed, the percentage jumped to 43 percent. Two goals that doctors hope to realize for their patients are in tension in this situation, the goal of ensuring that the patient is well informed about his options and the goal of sparing the patient from any unnecessary burdens. What would a good doctor do?

DOI: 10.4324/9781032640525-27

RESPONSES

The phenomenon giving rise to this dilemma for the doctor is known as the "nocebo effect," the flipside of the better-known placebo effect. A placebo effect, roughly, is a positive effect on the target disorder produced by the patient's *expectation* that the treatment process could be effective or by the patient's prior *conditioning* to certain features of the treatment process (Friesen 2020). A (pure) placebo, then, will be a treatment process each of whose positive effects are placebo effects. The nocebo effect can be analogously defined as a negative effect on the patient produced by the patient's expectation that the treatment process could have such an effect or by the patient's prior conditioning to certain features of the treatment process. In the case above, the doctor's worry is that disclosure of the possibility of sexual dysfunction will increase the likelihood that the patient will experience it. If the patient does experience dysfunction that would not have occurred but for this disclosure, this will count as a nocebo effect, since it would have been produced by the patient's expectation that the treatment process could have this side effect.

Doctors' concern for their patients' health and well-being motivates them to do what they can to encourage placebo effects and to discourage nocebo effects. Some ways of doing so are entirely unproblematic. For example, when a drug has beneficial non-placebo effects on the patient's condition, the fact that informing the patient of these effects would have an additional placebo effect on the patient is a good reason for disclosing that information to the patient. In the case of the nocebo effect, if there was no possibility of a certain side effect independently of a disclosure, then the doctor would not be withholding any information at all by not mentioning that side effect.

Other ways of managing these effects are not so obviously innocent. When the doctor wants to recommend a pure placebo whose benefits will derive entirely from the patient's expectations that it will be effective, it may not be necessary to *lie* to the patient (e.g., the doctor could say truthfully that the treatment has been shown to be effective without specifying how it was effective), but it will require deceiving the patient, since it is only if the patient (falsely) expects the process to be effective *independently* of their expectation that they will form that expectation (Groll 2011). Since deception is normally wrong and may also compromise the validity of the patient's consent to treatment it is difficult to justify administering pure placebos to patients.

By contrast with pure placebos, doctors can usually manage to avoid producing nocebo effects without employing lies or deception, since they only need to withhold information from the patient (Cohen 2012). Nevertheless, while it may be easier to justify withholding information than deceiving them, it does still need to be justified. Recall that in our example the doctor thought the patient would want to know of the risk of sexual dysfunction and was prepared to disclose it before learning about the nocebo effect. The tension between the values of minimizing risks and ensuring that the patient is fully informed is real. How should it be resolved?

On the old paternalistic model of the doctor–patient relationship (Emanuel 1992), information was to be delivered to the patient only when the doctor judged it to be in the patient's best interests. Assuming the doctor in our example is confident that Finasteride is the right treatment for this patient, then on this model the information about the possible sexual side effects may be withheld and even should be withheld, since clearly a 15 percent risk of these side effects is better for the patient than a 43 percent risk.

But the paternalistic model of the physician–patient relationship has been decisively rejected in medicine, in large part because it fails to acknowledge the importance of respecting patient autonomy. When the paternalistic model was still influential oncologists rarely disclosed cancer diagnoses to their patients on the grounds that delivering this news would cause needless suffering for their patients and possibly lower their chances of survival (Oken 1961). Since the 1970s it has been standard practice (in the West; see Chapter 3 for discussion of cultural variation here) to disclose cancer diagnoses on the grounds that competent patients are entitled to an accurate understanding of their medical situation so that they can make well-informed decisions about their treatment and their lives. If oncologists are required to disregard the potential negative effects of disclosing bad news to their patients, aren't doctors similarly required to disregard potential nocebo effects when deciding whether to disclose information about potential side effects?

Many would say yes. But in fact, the answer might be no, since the reasons for thinking respect for autonomy requires disclosing a diagnosis of cancer may not always carry over to disclosures with potential nocebo effects. Both the cancer patient and the patient with the enlarged prostate are *entitled* to the information that the doctor believes they may be better off without. But respect for autonomy only requires giving a patient the information they are entitled to if they want to receive it. Indeed, it would be paternalistic to force information on a patient they preferred not to have.

In the case of cancer patients, denying them information about their diagnosis may well be denying them information they would have wanted to have. It is far less certain that the patient with the enlarged prostate would want to know about the possibility of sexual dysfunction in light of the nocebo effect this information might produce, and the relatively low likelihood that they would reject this treatment to avoid this side effect.

The patient might want this information for other reasons, however. Patients don't just want information to ensure that their decisions about treatment reflect their values—they also have preferences about the way they reach those decisions. If patients normally prefer to deliberate using all relevant information, including information that would not alter their decision, there should be a presumption in favor of disclosing all relevant information to patients.

One way to override this presumption would be to ask the patient if they would be willing to waive their entitlement to the information with the nocebo effect potential (Miller and Colloca 2011). This request could avoid triggering the nocebo effect itself by soliciting general rather than specific consent to non-disclosure. For example, the patient could be told about nocebo effects in general and asked whether, in light of the potential for such an effect, they would prefer not to be informed about certain potential side effects of the medication that are not dangerous but could be annoying or frustrating. Whether this would work depends on whether general disclosures trigger nocebo effects of their own (Gelfand 2020). If they do, then we might want to consider whether a patient's hypothetical consent to both non-disclosure of the side effect *and* to not being asked to consent to non-disclosure would suffice for respecting their autonomy.

SUGGESTED READINGS

An important empirical study of the nocebo effect:

Mondaini, Nicola, Paolo Gontero, Gianluca Giubilei, Giuseppe Lombardi, Tommaso Cai, Andrea Gavazzi, and Riccardo Bartoletti. 2007. "Finasteride 5mg and Sexual Side Effects: How Many of These Are Related to a Nocebo Phenomenon?" *The Journal of Sexual Medicine* 4 (6): 1708–12.

On defining the placebo effect itself:

Friesen, Phoebe. 2020. "Towards an Account of the Placebo Effect." *Biology & Philosophy* 35 (1): 1–23.

Argues that expectation-based placebo effects require deception:

Groll, Daniel. 2011. "What You Don't Know Can Help You: The Ethics of Placebo Treatment." *Journal of Applied Philosophy* 28 (2): 188–202.

On how to strike a balance, on a case-by-case basis, between well-being of the patient and their desire for full disclosure:

Cohen, Shlomo. 2012. "The Nocebo Effect of Informed Consent." *Bioethics* 28 (3): 147– 54.

90 percent of a group of oncologists interviewed in 1961 preferred not to inform patients of a cancer diagnosis:

Oken, Donald. 1961. "What to Tell Cancer Patients: A Study of Medical Attitudes." *JAMA: The Journal of the American Medical Association* 175 (3): 1120–8.

Discusses the paternalistic model and three others:

Emanuel, Ezekiel J. and Linda L. Emanuel. 1992. "Four Models of the Physician–Patient Relationship." *JAMA: The Journal of the American Medical Association* 267 (16): 2221–6.

Recommends seeking authorization for withholding information that could have a nocebo effect as a way to reconcile concern for patient's well-being and informed consent:

Miller, Franklin G., and Luana Colloca. 2011. "The Placebo Phenomenon and Medical Ethics Rethinking the Relationship between Informed Consent and Risk–Benefit Assessment." *Theoretical Medicine and* Bioethics 32 (4): 229–43.

Raises concerns about the possible nocebo effects of seeking authorization for withholding information:

Gelfand, Scott. 2020. "The Nocebo Effect and Informed Consent—Taking Autonomy Seriously." *Cambridge Quarterly of Healthcare Ethics* 29 (2): 223–35.

PART VI

KILLING AND DYING

23

BETTER TO DIE?

The "Mercy" Killing at Memorial

THE CASE

Sometimes doctors are faced with situations in which it may seem that, no matter what choice they make, they will have done something seriously wrong.

Sheri Fink's book *Five Days at Memorial* (2013) recounts the tragic events that occurred at Memorial Medical Center in New Orleans shortly after Hurricane Katrina. When the hurricane hit on a Monday in the summer of 2005 there were over 2,000 people bunking at the Memorial Medical Center, including around 200 patients and 600 staff members. On Tuesday the levees failed, flooding the city. Memorial started evacuating patients by boat and helicopter, but when Memorial's backup generators failed on Wednesday, leaving the hospital without lights, air conditioning, and running water, there were still over 100 patients, including several who had been on mechanical ventilators and now needed to be ventilated by hand. Many of the sickest were bedbound and on the seventh floor, which meant that evacuating them by helicopter would require carrying them down several flights of stairs and then up several more flights of stairs to the helipad.

The staff decided to sort the remaining patients into three groups in order of priority for evacuation. The highest priority group, the "1s,"

DOI: 10.4324/9781032640525-29

were patients in decent health that could sit up or walk. Next were the "2s," those who were less healthy and less mobile than the "1s," and finally the "3s," who were patients that were either very sick or had "do not resuscitate" or "DNR" orders.

On Thursday, as the 1s and the 2s were being evacuated, the police announced that everyone who could leave the building had to leave that evening. There was unrest elsewhere in the city and the police could no longer guard the hospital. It was highly doubtful that the 3s could be evacuated by that deadline. Since the staff were being evacuated these very sick patients would be left without care and protection for at least one night and possibly much longer. This prompted a conversation about euthanasia among a small group of doctors which led to a very fateful decision. The details of what happened next are uncertain, but when the doctors left that evening they were able to say that they had left no living patients behind. According to a later toxicology report, 18 of those patients died with high doses of morphine and midazolam in their systems.

One of these patients was Emmett Everett, 61, who was 380 pounds, paraplegic, and awaiting colostomy surgery when Katrina hit. Everett had fed himself breakfast Thursday morning and was feeling fine except for some dizzy spells. Earlier he had told a nurse "Don't leave me behind" and did not have a DNR. Dr. Pou told the nurses on the seventh floor that she was going to give Emmett something for his dizziness and likely told Everett the same thing before giving him a lethal injection.

Another patient was Janice Burgess, 79, who was 350 pounds, had advanced uterine cancer and kidney failure, and had a DNR order. She was expected to die in the next day or two and was only receiving palliative care. Since she had already been sedated to unconsciousness with morphine, she was not uncomfortable, but Dr. Thiele was concerned that after the staff had left the morphine would wear off and she would spend her last hours in agony. Dr. Thiele decided to increase her morphine dosage significantly and she was dead within minutes.

RESPONSES

The doctors who actively "euthanized" (i.e., killed) those patients believed that the patients could not be evacuated and that if they were left alone the pain-relieving drugs they were on would wear off and the patients would die miserable deaths. If those beliefs were correct, then many would argue that lethal injections were in the patients' best interests. Death may be bad for us whenever it comes, but sometimes it prevents something even worse. Still, we can ask: would the fact that the lethal injections were in the patients' best interests be enough on its own to justify those injections?

One potential objection is that the only reason lethal injections were in the patients' best interests is that doctors had decided to leave the hospital and to stop administering comfort care. Doctors, so the thought goes, have a professional duty not to abandon their patients and cannot use their decision to violate that duty in order to justify giving lethal injections. In defense of the doctors, however, it could be argued that the limits to the duty not to abandon patients had been exceeded in this disaster (Kipnis 2007). The police had warned the staff that they would no longer be protecting the hospital and even ordered everyone to leave who could. Remaining in the hospital under such circumstances might go beyond the limits of doctors' duty to accept risks on behalf of their patients.

A second potential objection is that although it may sometimes be permissible to withhold life-sustaining treatment and even to withdraw it, these doctors *killed* their patients and there is an absolute prohibition on actions that lead to the death of innocent and non-threatening persons, even when death comes as a benefit to them. However, there is general agreement that sometimes causing a patient to die is permissible so long as the doctor does not intend the patient's death. This view is also reflected in the law. For example, when a patient is being taken off a ventilator to die, it was the usual practice at Memorial and elsewhere to administer morphine to prevent the patient from suffering the agony of breath hunger as they died. The amount of morphine needed to prevent breath hunger also tended to hasten the patient's death, but this was merely an anticipated side effect of the morphine, not something the doctors intended (Fink 2013).

This distinction between intending and merely foreseeing a patient's death (a distinction that plays a key role in the "Doctrine of Double Effect") is the basis for a third potential objection to the Memorial doctors' lethal injections. According to this objection, there is an absolute prohibition on acting or omitting to act while intending death as a means or as an end, although it can be permissible to act or omit to act while merely foreseeing that death will be the result

(Sullivan 1976). The distinction between results that are intended and those which are merely foreseen corresponds roughly to the distinction between those results an agent needs to occur to achieve their goals in acting or omitting to act and those results they do not need to occur.

We know that the Memorial doctors acted with the goals of relieving and preventing pain. The question now is whether they intended the death of the patient as the means to realizing any of those goals. If they had used a paralytic instead of morphine and sedatives, it would be obvious they intended the patients' deaths, since a paralytic, unlike those other drugs, can only prevent pain by causing death. Even so, there are other indications that they intended the deaths, such as the fact that they gave large doses of morphine to patients who were not currently in pain, like Everett and Burgess, and excessively high doses to others who were in pain. Why did they do this? One of their aims in delivering those injections was to prevent future pain—the pain and suffering the patients were in danger of experiencing after the doctors had left the hospital. It's clear that the way they intended those injections to prevent that future pain and suffering was by ending the patients' lives.

An absolute prohibition on intending death is more widely accepted than one on killing, but this prohibition too has been challenged. (See Chapters 16 and 44 for more on the significance of intentions.) One way is by arguing that that the distinction between intending and merely foreseeing harm is always morally irrelevant (Thomson 1999; but see Hanser 2005). But that is not the only way. Here is another challenge (Kamm 1997). When a doctor amputates a patient's limb to save their life, the doctor harms the patient and intends that lesser harm as a means of preventing the greater harm of death. This is often permissible. If it is sometimes permissible to intend a lesser harm to prevent a greater harm, and death is sometimes necessary to prevent a greater harm, why would it never be permissible to intend death?

Many ethicists reject both an absolute constraint on killing and on intending death. But these constraints are not the only possible grounds for objecting to the lethal injections. Almost everyone would agree that it is wrong to kill (or even treat) a competent patient without their free and informed consent. Dr. Pou delivered a lethal injection to Emmitt Everett, who was alert and probably competent. He may have consented to the injection; however, if he was only told the injection was for his dizziness, then Dr. Pou obtained his consent by wrongfully withholding crucial information from him, which would invalidate it. Janice Burgess, on the other hand, was unconscious and would die within a day or two anyway. Unless there was a good reason to believe that she would not have wanted to be euthanized in this situation, Dr. Thiel's decision to cause her death seems more justifiable than Dr. Pou's decision to cause Everett's.

SUGGESTED READINGS

The authoritative account of the events at Memorial, which has since been made into a TV miniseries:

> Fink, Sheri. 2013. *Five Days at Memorial: Life and Death in a Storm-Ravaged Hospital.* New York: Crown Publishers.

An account of physicians' duties not to abandon their patients and an application to Memorial:

> Kipnis, Kenneth. 2007. "Forced Abandonment and Euthanasia: A Question from Katrina." *Social Research: An International Quarterly* 74 (1): 79–100.

For an argument that sometimes it is impossible to avoid serious wrongdoing and that the doctors at Memorial may have been in such a situation, even if euthanizing patients who could not consent was morally better than abandoning them, see:

> Tessman, Lisa. 2017. *When Doing the Right Things Is Impossible.* Oxford: Oxford University Press.

For a defense of an absolute prohibition against acting or omitting to act while intending the death that results, see:

> Sullivan, Thomas D. 1976. "Active and Passive Euthanasia: An Impertinent Distinction?" *The Human Life Review* 3 (3): 40–6.

Challenges existence of both an absolute prohibition on killing and an absolute prohibition on intending someone's death, and also makes influential arguments against the significance of intentions to permissibility:

> Thomson, Judith Jarvis. 1999. "Physician-Assisted Suicide: Two Moral Arguments." *Ethics* 109: 497–518.

Defends the moral significance of intentions against Thomson's influential objections:

> Hanser, Matthew. 2005. "Permissibility and Practical Inference." *Ethics* 115 (3): 443–70.

For an accessible defense of both the killing/letting die and the intended/foreseen distinction:

> Kamm, Frances. 1997. "The Right to Choose Death." *Boston Review*, June 1.

TO KILL, OR LET DIE?
Rachels on Active and Passive Euthanasia

THE CASE

Since the 1980s, it's become standard practice for physicians to respect requests from patients to stop life-preserving care, removing life-support devices in ways all but certain to lead to the death of the patient. Other medical actions that lead to death, especially *euthanasia* and *assisted suicide*, remain much less common, and much more controversial. The difference, it can seem, is that, even though both withdrawing (or withholding) care and providing medical aid in dying lead to death, the latter involves *killing* the patient (or at least assisting in killing) while the former only involves *letting them die* of the underlying disease. And, we might think, for physicians especially, there are much stronger duties (of "non-maleficence") against killing than against mere "letting them die."

James Rachels (1975) presents a pair of cases that are intended to shake our confidence in the moral relevance of the distinction between killing and letting die—and thus our confidence that there is a deep moral difference between medical killings, like euthanasia, and medical lettings-to-die, like standard withdrawals of lifesaving care.

> **Smith**: Smith stands to inherit a large fortune if his 6-year-old cousin does not survive to adulthood. Smith walks into the

DOI: 10.4324/9781032640525-30

bathroom planning to kill his cousin, sees his cousin playing in the bath, and forcibly drowns him, making it look like an accident.

Jones: Jones also stands to inherit a large fortune if his 6-year-old cousin does not survive to adulthood. Jones walks into the bath-room, planning to kill his cousin, sees his cousin playing in the bath, but does not need to forcibly drown him: his cousin slips, hits his head, and passes; all he has to do is watch him drown.

The only difference between these cases appears to be that Smith actively *kills* his cousin, whereas Jones passively *lets him die*. Yet what Smith does seems to be no worse than what Jones does. So, Rachels invites us to infer, there is no basic or intrinsic moral difference between killing and letting die. Thus, we are meant to conclude, "active" euthanasia, intentionally killing or assisting in it, is not intrin-sically or basically worse than the much more widely accepted practice of passive euthanasia, where we merely let patients die.

RESPONSES

There are two basic responses one can make to Rachels' argument here—either deny his conclusions about his thought experiment; or deny that the results generalize to the real-world moral problem of euthanasia.

Philosophers have resisted Rachels on the thought experiment itself in various ways. One is to deny that what Smith and Jones do, the letting die and the killing, really are morally equivalent. How would we know they are both *equally* bad? Both are really quite awful, beyond the point of awfulness where we normally bother to make moral distinctions. But that does not mean there are no differences, here. Our reluctance to draw distinctions may simply reflect a high degree of revulsion to both, and also the fact that such distinctions are normally not necessary—Smith and Jones should both go to prison, possibly for life.

Another line of response to the thought experiment is to resist the idea that the only difference between Smith and Jones is that Smith kills his cousin while Jones merely allows him to die. Here is one difference. Jones and Smith have different options: Jones feels "fortunate" that he does not have to drown his cousin to get the money, while Smith is "unlucky" in that he lacks the option of sitting back and letting his cousin die. Jones, the letter-die, has the option to inherit the money without killing, while Smith, the killer, does not. This difference might not seem significant, but imagine that Smith had had the same option, while keeping everything else the same (that is, keeping it the same that he killed). If (like Jones) he could have let die instead of killed, killing would have been much worse than letting die (awful as that would have been), killing would be grotesque, and gratuitous, something that would require not just extreme greed but sadistic cruelty besides (Hill 2018; see also Kamm 2007.)

This brings us to a methodological concern about the deployment of the original thought experiment. Some philosophers argue that the distinction between killing and letting die might make a difference in other cases, even if doesn't make a difference here. To illustrate this, we can borrow a case from Phillipa Foot (1967). Suppose that paramedics are rushing to a scene to save a group of people critically injured in a large car accident. In one scenario they pass a dying man on the side of the road, but do not stop so they can save even more at the accident site. Letting this man die, in order to save more, may or may not be permissible, but it would very clearly be impermissible to kill him in order to save the same group—say, if he were healthy and in the middle of the road, but had to be run over to get there. Thus, the distinction seems to make a difference in this case, even if not in Rachels'. Foot's case does not necessarily establish that there *is* a difference between killing and letting die, since there may be other differences here—say, between having the death be part of the plan and having it be a mere side effect of it. But it does something to undermine the form of argument that Rachels uses here. That a factor does not make a difference, alone, does not show that it does not make a difference in combination with other factors (Thomson 1976; Kagan 1989: 259).

This methodological moral matters to the bioethical context for Rachels' case. There are many differences between cases where doctors actually kill patients or help them kill themselves and patients where they let them die by agreeing to withhold life-extending treatments. Some of these differences may matter in themselves: it may be that active euthanasia is more likely to be abused, resulting in non-consensual killing, or that active euthanasia more than passive euthanasia undermines important cultural norms around the sanctity of life and our proper authority over it.

Other differences, however, may modulate the importance of the very distinction between activity and passivity itself. Doctors, for instance, may have special reason to avoid causing harm, beyond their reasons to provide the best treatment they can. If so, then even if killing and letting die are equivalent for some cases not involve doctors and patients, in medical cases they are not. Or perhaps not; this argument would rest on the claim that performing active euthanasia is harming the patient—exactly what patients requesting the procedure would deny, thinking continued life in their condition a harm and the end of it a benefit. Conversely, it may be that it matters whether death is desired or consented to—that where someone wants to die, and agrees to, it is no worse, or not much worse, to kill or help kill them to let them die (Dworkin et al. 1997). In that case active euthanasia might be permissible, but the Smith and Jones case would not help us show that it is. Even if Rachels is wrong that the distinction between killing and letting die never matters, it may still turn out that it does not matter in the medical cases he cares most about.

SUGGESTED READINGS

For the original case, see:
> Rachels, James. 1975. "Active and Passive Euthanasia." *New England Journal of Medicine*, January 9. https://doi.org/10.1056/NEJM197501092920206.

For arguments that Smith's actions are actually worse, see:
> Hill, Scott. 2018. "Murdering an Accident Victim: A New Objection to the Bare-Difference Argument." *Australasian Journal of Philosophy* 96 (4): 767–78. https://doi.org/10.1080/00048402.2017.1414275.

> Kamm, Frances. 2007. *Intricate Ethics: Rights, Responsibilities, and Permissible Harm.* New York: Oxford University Press. https://doi.org/10.1093/acprof: oso/9780195189698.001.0001.

For Foot's rescue case, see:
> Foot, Philippa. 1967. "The Problem of Abortion and the Doctrine of the Double Effect." *Oxford Review* 5: 5–15. https://philarchive.org/rec/ FOOTPO-2

For the concern that Rachels' case does not show that there is no general distinction between killing and letting die:
> Thomson, Judith Jarvis. 1976. "Killing, Letting Die, and the Trolley Problem." *The Monist* 59 (2): 204–17. https://doi.org/10.5840/monist197659224.

Kagan, Shelly. 1989. *The Limits of Morality*. New York: Oxford University Press. https://doi.org/10.1093/0198239165.001.0001.

For the claim that the distinction does not matter, when the death is the result of a consensual process, see:

Dworkin, Ronald, Thomas Nagel, Robert Nozick, John Rawls, Thomas Scanlon, and Judith Jarvis Thomson. 1997. "Assisted Suicide: The Philosophers' Brief." *The New York Review of Books*, March, 41–7

WHAT DOES IT MEAN TO KILL?

Stopping Hearts, Artificial and Otherwise

THE CASE

Bioethics, or at least a large part of it, is about what we can do to people's bodies. Yet, we rarely consider when and why something counts as a part of the body. New medical technologies raise these issues particularly sharply—and in a way that should make us think even harder about what it is to kill and what to let die.

Millions of people across the word rely on implantable medical devices like pacemakers and implantable cardiac defibrillators (ICDs). These devices are prescribed and implanted by expert physicians to prolong life; usually, patients are happy to have them. But some people do ask to have them deactivated or even taken out (Kramer et al. 2012). Most often, this is an end-of-life measure, meant to hasten death or just to prevent suffering from increasingly frequent and decreasingly effective shocks. In rare instances, however, young and otherwise-healthy patients have asked to have these vital prostheses deactivated and removed. Consider the following, based on a particularly wrenching real-world case, from Canada (Pullman and Hodgkinson 2016):

A 29-year-old patient—we can call him "Pat"—required an implantable defibrillator to treat a serious congenital heart disease that could cause his heart to spontaneously stop beating, requiring a shock

DOI: 10.4324/9781032640525-31

to restart it. Although the device had fired twice, presumably saving him in both cases from a serious cardiac arrest, Pat did not believe he needed it. And he found the wires visible under his skin unsightly and embarrassing. Pat asked to have his defibrillator deactivated and removed, despite warnings that without it he would be at very high risk of a life-threatening heart attack. Eventually, the device was taken out, and Pat did indeed suffer a heart attack (as it turned out, he survived, but with significant cognitive impairments). The device was later re-implanted.

Should Pat's doctors have acceded to his request? Some of them, and the Canadian courts, seem to have seen this as an unusual but ultimately straightforward case of *refusal of care* (Pullman and Hodgkinson 2016); Pat was entitled to the deactivation and removal of this device for the same reason that any patient is entitled to stop ongoing mechanical interventions in their body. Others involved, including the physician who implanted the device, refused to be involved in removing it. They may have had various reasons for doing so, including concerns about whether he was truly competent to make this life-altering decision for himself. Or—and this concern will be the focus of this entry—they may have simply not wanted to be involved in this way in the patient's death. Some reasonable physicians, after all, might see this as less like shutting off a patient's external life support, and more like stopping their heart—a measure that most physicians would and should oppose, in all but the rare and specific circumstances that might (arguably) justify euthanasia or assisted suicide.

RESPONSES

How can we tell whether removing or deactivating implantable devices is more like withdrawing care, on a competent request, or more like assisting in a suicidally risky activity? That is, how can we know whether this is a matter of *killing*, or merely *allowing* to die (assuming that distinction itself matters; see Chapter 24)? The answer seems to depend on the character of the rights that patients have regarding their devices. If those rights are like rights regarding other technology used in medical care, then they preclude continuing care without consent. If they are more like our rights regarding our own body, then patients have no more right to ask a doctor to remove a

true even if there is no antecedent special relationship between you and Ana, such as parent–child, friendship, or doctor–patient. Why might this be? Notice that if we treat Ana, we can predict the identity of the person whose life we will have saved, namely, Ana's. In other words, the beneficiary of treating Ana is *identified*. But if we vaccinate the group of healthy people, while we can expect to save someone's life that way, we have no way to predict whose life that will be. The beneficiary of the vaccine will be, in this sense, merely *statistical* rather than identified.

Our preference for saving identified persons may not only explain why we would prefer to save Ana, but also some of our spending priorities as a society, such as our greater investments in treatments like antiretroviral therapy and dialysis even when preventive measures would save more (statistical) lives per dollar. But is this preference also morally defensible?

RESPONSES

Here is one uncontroversial way in which the difference between identified and statistical persons could matter morally. Sometimes the reason the identities of the potential beneficiaries of an intervention cannot be predicted in advance is because the benefits will not be received until some point in the distant future, either because the potential beneficiaries do not yet exist or because they are not yet sick. The timing of the benefit may not matter on its own, but it can make a difference to the probability that the benefits will occur, which does matter. The scarcity might turn out to only be temporary, and even if enduring the forecasted threats might not materialize (Fried 1969).

This defense of the preference for saving identified lives may be fine as far as it goes, but it cannot justify that preference in all the situations in which we display it. We continue to prefer saving identified lives even in situations in which prioritizing statistical lives over identified lives would maximize the expected number of lives saved. One such situation is exemplified by the case above. Even though the vaccines are less likely than the treatment to save the lives of the people it reaches, they are still expected to save more lives because they will reach more people. Yet we still prefer to save Ana, the identified person.

It is initially puzzling how it could make any moral sense, in the absence of special ties, to bring about lower total benefits than we could with our resources. Shouldn't we always try to get the most bang for our buck? But there is a familiar value that does sometimes require that we do less good than we could, namely fairness. Fairness demands that we aid those with the strongest claims to assistance before those with weaker claims, even when satisfying the weaker claims would yield the greatest benefits (Broome 1984).

How much someone needs a resource, as measured by how badly off they would be without it, is commonly taken to be relevant to the strength of their claim to it. For example, if we have the resources to either relieve the headaches of many people or to save the life of one person, fairness requires us to save the life, even if our resources could relieve so many headaches that the total benefit produced by those resources would be larger.

In cases like Ana's above, however, we are not deciding between relieving headaches and saving lives—we are deciding between two *lifesaving* interventions. And the death of someone whose identity cannot be predicted in advance is not, for that reason, any less bad for the victim. It may be impossible for us to know who would have died without a vaccination, but whoever it is, they are just as flesh-and-blood as Ana and have a life that is just as precious to them as Ana's life is to her. Not only is there no apparent reason to think fairness would demand treating Ana instead of vaccinating the many, treating Ana may even be unfair to whoever will die without the vaccine. If their claim to assistance is as strong as Ana's, then shouldn't everyone be given an equal chance of assistance by, for example, flipping a coin to decide between treating Ana and vaccinating the group?

Those who would defend our preference for saving identified lives suggest that, although it is true that the deaths of Ana and of those who would die without the vaccine are equally bad, this overlooks an important difference between Ana and the healthy people who need vaccination. Her claim is not stronger because her death would be any worse than the deaths of those, whoever they are, who would die without vaccination. It is stronger because, given the evidence available to those deciding whom to help, she faces a 100 percent risk of death without the treatment whereas the healthy people who need vaccination face only a 1 percent risk of death without it. Since someone facing a high risk of death would be in a worse position without assistance than anyone facing a low risk of death, Ana has a stronger claim to treatment than the healthy people have to vaccination (Frick 2015). Even though vaccination would be expected to save more lives, fairness demands that we prioritize reducing Ana's high risk of death over reducing healthy people's already low risk of death.

The choice between assisting Ana, who is identifiable, and the healthy people, who are not, is also a choice between treatment (medicine for Ana) and prevention (vaccines for the healthy). As a society we tend to spend much more on treatment than on prevention. This spending preference is often criticized on the grounds that prevention is more cost-effective. Would the justification just given for preferring identified over statistical lives also vindicate this policy preference?

Not necessarily. Sometimes the beneficiaries of treatment are statistical and sometimes the beneficiaries of prevention are identifiable. We can understand treatments as interventions intended to help someone who already has symptomatic disease or injury, and preventive measures as interventions intended to prevent symptomatic disease or injury (for a reasonable length of time) in someone who is susceptible to it, such as immunizations, chlorinated water, and screenings for pre-symptomatic disease (Faust and Menzel 2012). When we try to treat people who already have symptomatic disease, we will normally be able to identify who would have lost their life without treatment. But if using our resources to invest in the means to treat people who will suffer from the disease at some point in the future would also be considered treatment, the justification above for privileging identifiable victims would not carry over to this form of treatment, since its beneficiaries are merely statistical. Moreover, sometimes the beneficiaries of preventive measures are identifiable. Adding chlorine to the water in an area with cholera would prevent harm to identifiable people, specifically nearly everyone who uses the water in the area.

SUGGESTED READINGS

Argues in favor of favoring identified lives:
> Daniels, Norman. 2015. "Can There Be Moral Force to Favoring an Identified Over a Statistical Life?" In I. Glenn Cohen, Norman Daniels, and Nir Eyal (eds.), *Identified Versus Statistical Lives: An Interdisciplinary Perspective* (pp. 110–23). Oxford: Oxford University Press.

Classic article on statistical versus identified lives:

Fried, Charles. 1969. "The Value of Life." *Harvard Law Review* 82 (7): 1415–37.

Influential account of comparative fairness:

Broome, John. 1984. "Selecting People Randomly." *Ethics* 95 (1): 38–55.

Defends prioritizing identifiable lives over statistical lives, other things equal, on the grounds that identifiable lives are at greater epistemic risk:

Frick, Johann. 2015. "Treatment Versus Prevention in the Fight Against HIV/AIDS and the Problem of Identified Versus Statistical Lives." In I. Glenn Cohen, Norman Daniels, and Nir Eyal (eds.), *Identified Versus Statistical Lives: An Interdisciplinary Perspective* (pp. 182–202). Oxford: Oxford University Press.

Useful analysis of the distinction between treatment and prevention:

Faust, Halley S., and Paul T. Menzel. 2012. "Introduction." In *Prevention vs. Treatment: What's the Right Balance?* (pp. 1–33). Oxford: Oxford University Press.

Argues that what is morally relevant is the risk that *someone* will suffer a certain harm, not (as Frick claims) the risk that this or that individual will suffer that harm:

Otsuka, Michael. 2015. "Risking Life and Limb: How to Discount Harms by Their Improbability." In I. Glenn Cohen, Norman Daniels, and Nir Eyal (eds.), *Identified Versus Statistical Lives: An Interdisciplinary Perspective* (pp. 182–202). Oxford: Oxford University Press.

WHAT DOES IT MEAN TO DIE, I?
Jahi McMath and the Definition of Death

THE CASE

What is it for a human person to die? The tragic case of Jahi McMath vividly illustrates important philosophical and bioethical controversies on this essential question.

On January 3, 2014, Jahi McMath a 13-year-old girl from Oakland, California, was declared dead—the first time. Jahi had experienced uncontrolled bleeding as a complication of a routine tonsillectomy. Her condition quickly worsened and she eventually became unresponsive to repeated neurological exams, though her heart continued to beat and some respiratory functions continued, albeit with mechanical assistance. Eventually her physicians diagnosed a loss of all brain function—sufficient for death under the laws of the state of California. Her mother, Nailah Winkfield, refused to accept that the warm body in the bed was her daughter's corpse. She sued the hospital, which was preparing to withdraw life support. Eventually, her family was allowed to move Jahi from the hospital in California to a facility in New Jersey, where state law blocks declaration of death on the basis of neurological evidence in some cases where the patient or their family disagree. Jahi—or, depending on who you ask, her *body*—continued to be warm, with a beating heart, for almost five more

DOI: 10.4324/9781032640525-33

years, until she (or her body) died by any definition, on June 22, 2018 (Shewmon and Salomon 2021).

Jahi's case illustrates a debate about the definition of death that has raged since the invention of sophisticated artificial life support technologies in the 1960s. Prior to that time, death was determined by a cardio-respiratory standard—we died when our heart and lungs irreversibly ceased to function. Artificial ventilation and related technologies, however, made it possible for a person's heart to continue beating after all of their brain functions had ceased. Physicians began to be concerned that treating effectively brainless bodies as living persons was a waste of intensive care resources that could be devoted to saving the lives of people with a chance at recovery. Moreover, the practice of waiting for the heart and lungs to stop moving before declaring death made it more difficult to carry out patients' wishes to donate their organs to living recipients in need of them. And scientists increasingly argued that, practical matters aside, the loss of all brain function simply is human death, since the brain is what unites all of the disparate parts of the human body into a single coherent organism. Proponents of the brain-based standard for death won the resulting policy debates, leading to the passage of laws in states like McMath's California allowing death to be diagnosed by neurological criteria.

RESPONSES

Jahi McMath's case intensified debates about the nature of death and about our policies around it. Some ethicists took it as an occasion to reiterate arguments that massive loss of brain function makes a person profoundly disabled, without killing them (Truog and Miller 2014). They point, among other things, to the fact that Jahi's body, maintained on a ventilator, continued to do many of the things that the bodies of living human organisms do, including processing and metabolizing nutrients, puberty and eventually menstruation. Critics of brain-based death use this as one of many examples to illustrate how many apparently "integrating" or whole-body processes can continue even after the loss of all neurological functioning in the brain, including the brain stem (Shewmon 2018). They argue that what makes a human organism a human organism is the ability of its organs to work together to provide energy to and remove waste products from its cells, a process that is accomplished primarily by the circulatory system, not the brain. Thus, they argue, human life does not necessarily end exactly at the moment all brain function has irreversibly ceased.

Other philosophers have argued, in response, that both the legally enshrined brain-based view and the traditional cardio-respiratory view illicitly assume that we should define the death of a human being in terms of the lifespan of a human *animal* or *organism*. Many philosophers, by contrast, have argued that we human beings are not animals but something more like embodied *minds* or *persons*: that we come into existence when we gain the capacity for thought and/or feeling, and go out of it when we lose that capacity (see Chapter 2, Green and Wikler 1980). Others have argued that whatever the case may be about what sorts of beings we are, the loss of the ability to consciously think or feel means that we are dead for all practical purposes, since moral principles giving us claims on medical resources or forbidding doctors to give our vital organs to others no longer apply (Veatch 2005). Both views would imply not only that brain-dead patients like Jahi are dead, but also that patients who (unlike) Jahi can breathe on their own, but who have permanently lost consciousness, are also (at least, legally) dead. This "higher-brain," as opposed to *whole-brain*, definition of death, though popular among philosophers, has not been adopted in any jurisdiction: people simply seem to have a hard time believing that a warm body, breathing on its own, is actually a corpse. Most jurisdictions, including California and all US states, stick instead to some version of the "whole-brain" definition, though controversy continues as to how this could be made philosophically and medically tenable.

Jahi's case also involves controversies that are less philosophical, and controversies that go beyond the definition of death. Jahi's family did not believe that she had even lost the capacity for consciousness. They later produced video which, they claim, showed that she was able to move her limbs in response to communication from her family; some experts, but not others, take this to demonstrate that she had never lost all brain function at all, and indeed would not have been dead even by the "higher-brain" standard (Shewmon and Solomon 2021). If they are right, then something must have been wrong either with the conduct of the initial exams (though Shewmon and Solomon argue they were conducted according to accepted protocols) or with the procedures that define which clinical findings are sufficient to demonstrate whole-brain death.

Concerns about Jahi's care, in particular, brings us to a context broader than, though related to, the issues around the definition of death. Jahi's family was reluctant to accept her doctor's claim that she had died partly because her death itself during routine surgery was so surprising, and partly because of a history of mistrust of the medical system. Though patients of all backgrounds sometimes have catastrophic complications from routine procedures, troubling evidence emerging that this is more common, for many procedures, in patients from marginalized groups—particularly, in the US, African Americans (Goodwin 2018). This raises obvious issues of justice in the delivery of healthcare. A history of health inequity also likely shaped their response to the diagnosis of death itself, given how the bodies of African Americans have been (at worst) abused and exploited (see Chapters 29 and 34), and (at best) neglected (Chapters 34, 36, 37), by the American medical establishment.

SUGGESTED READINGS

For a medically sophisticated take on the facts in Jahi's story:

Shewmon, D Alan, and Noriko Salamon. 2021. "The Extraordinary Case of Jahi Mcmath." *Perspectives in Biology and Medicine* 64 (4): 457–78. https://doi.org/10.1353/pbm.2021.0036

The adoption of brain-based standards for death nationwide was strongly influenced by the following report:

President's Commission for the Study of Ethical Problems in Medicine and Biomedical and Behavioral Research. 1981. "Defining Death."

For criticism of brain-based death, arguing that the McMath case should push us back towards a cardiorespiratory definition:

Shewmon, D. Alan. 2018. "The Case of Jahi McMath: A Neurologist's View." *Hastings Center Report* 48 (6): S74–6. https://doi.org/10.1007/s12028-018-0593-x.

Truog, Robert D., and Franklin G. Miller. 2014. "Changing the Conversation about Brain Death." *American Journal of Bioethics* 14 (8): 9–14. https://doi.org/10.1080/15265161.2014.925154.

For a defense of brain death, despite the concerns in the case:

Magnus, David C., Benjamin S. Wilfond, and Arthur L. Caplan. 2014. "Accepting Brain Death." *New England Journal of Medicine* 370 (10): 891–94. https://doi.org/10.1056/NEJMp1400930.

For the alternative, personhood-based or "higher-brain" view:

Green, Michael B., and Daniel Wikler. 1980. "Brain Death and Personal Identity." *Philosophy & Public Affairs* 9 (2): 105–33. http://www.jstor.org/stable/2265108

Veatch, Robert M. 2005. "The Death of Whole-Brain Death: The Plague of the Disaggregators, Somaticists, and Mentalists." *Journal of Medicine and Philosophy* 30 (4): 353–78. https://doi.org/10.1080/03605310591008504.

And on the social and racial justice context for Jahi's case, see:

Goodwin, Michele. 2018. "Revisiting Death: Implicit Bias and the Case of Jahi McMath." *The Hastings Center Report* 48 Suppl. 4 (November): S77–80. https://doi.org/10.1002/hast.963.

WHAT DOES IT MEAN TO DIE, II?

Death and the Sanctity of the Body in Islam

THE CASE

Religious beliefs often deeply influence all parties to bioethical dilemmas, providing ethical resources as well as potentially problematic ritual constraints. Take, for instance, the treatment of the dead in contexts of shared Islamic faith.

Suppose Fatemeh, a 40-year-old woman living in Iran, has agreed to be an organ donor. Unfortunately, Fatemeh is involved in a serious car accident and has lost all brain function. Zahra, 46, is a patient with heart failure, in need of a heart transplant, in the same hospital. Fatemeh's husband supports the procedure, but her parents do not.

According to tradition, the Prophet Muhammad said that, "Breaking a bone of a dead person is like breaking a bone of a living person" (Sachedina 2009). If, analogously, "cutting out the heart" of a dead person is like "cutting out the heart" of a living person, Fatemeh's parents reason, then it would be un-Islamic, and thus morally wrong, to proceed. Urgently needing to start the procedure, while Fatemeh's organs are still in good condition, the physicians in the hospital request an ethics consultation. They want to know what they should do: whether the Islamic ethical tradition that all parties, including Fatemeh, subscribe to, allows or forbids organ extraction in this case.

DOI: 10.4324/9781032640525-34

RESPONSES

Fatemeh's case reveals several significant issues concerning the treatment of the dead in the Islamic tradition. Considering how these issues arise can help us to see distinctive features of Islamic bioethics, relative to the secular perspective that informs most of the entries in this book.

One of these features is certainly the role of religious tradition. All Islamic bioethicists attribute substantial authority to revelation, though as in many religious traditions there is substantial disagreement as to what exactly the sources of revelation are. All Islamic bioethicists recognize the authority of the Quran itself, and many also recognize non-Quranic sources like the aforementioned sayings of the Prophet or the divinely guided rulings of historical religious authorities. Even thus supplemented, however, Islamic revelation does not give detailed, determinate answers to every ethical question that arises in modern medical practice.

Revelation is particularly in need of supplementation where, as here, ethical questions concern recently developed technologies. Artificial life support and transplantation of vital organs were unknown at the writing of the Quran and the most widely accepted later sources. Thus recourse to tradition here must operate by appeal to analogies or deeper principles. In Fatemeh's case, these sources would have to address several questions. First, is Fatemeh dead, so that we should think of transplanting her organs as analogous to dismembering a corpse? If so, second, could it nonetheless be justifiable? If not, if Fatemeh is alive, could it (third) be permissible to end her life, profoundly limited as it now is, in order to save Zahra's?

The definition of death is as hotly debated in the Islamic world as it has been in the West (see Chapter 27). Islam defines death in the first instance as the total separation of the soul (*nafs*) from the body. But there is no consensus on when this occurs. Some authorities on Islamic law have argued that since death is a biological process, this would be a question for biomedical science—and thus that, if there was a global scientific consensus that death was loss of brain function, then Islamic law could assume that the soul leaves the body at brain death (Miller et al. 2014). But some authors, citing traditional Islamic metaphysics, argue that, since the soul is intimately associated with air, we cannot assume it has left until breathing has permanently stopped (Bedir and Aksoy 2011).

Defining death does not settle the issue in discussions of the Islamic tradition. Some scholars who oppose brain-based definitions of death, on Islamic grounds, argue that this need not preclude transplanting organs from people whose brains have lost all function but whose bodies are kept alive by artificial life support. In doing so, they reject what in the West is called the "dead donor rule," the idea that if organ donors are not already dead then taking vital organs wrongfully kills them (Truog and Miller 2008). Muslim scholars argue, by contrast, that in certain narrowly defined circumstances killing might some-times be acceptable, since the person in question is very close to death and doing so serves the holy purpose of preserving life. Here ethicists can draw on a long tradition in Islam of understanding death as a pro-cess, involving an intermediate stage of "unstable life" that is different from "stable life" in ethically significant ways (Sachedina 2009). That state may be reached when all brain function is lost, even if the process of death has not been fully completed. This reasoning may support a practice of extracting organs while a body is still being maintained on life support, whether that body is considered fully dead or not.

Suppose, however, that we think Fatemeh is fully dead. In the West, laws and prevailing ethical guidelines would make the permissibil-ity of transplantation fairly clear, presuming her prior authorization (though in practice, the family's opposition might make physicians reluctant to proceed). But recall that Fatemeh's parents are concerned about a distinctively Islamic proscription against dismembering dead human bodies. Scholars, however, point to aspects of the tradition that allow damage to corpses, for sufficiently important purposes (Chamsi-Pasha & Albar, 2021). In particular, there is a long tradition that allows making incision to save a living child when their mother has died during pregnancy or childbirth (Sachedina 2009). The justification is that doing so is necessary to preserve life, so that the evil of the desecration is outweighed by a greater good. Many Muslims believe the same or similar logic applies to organ transplantation after death: that there is something bad about cutting into a corpse, to extract an organ for transplant, but that if this organ is necessary to preserve a life, like Zahra's, then this good might outweigh the bad of desecration and make it permissible to proceed on balance (Padela & Auda, 2020).

Still, others argue that God's ownership of the body, or the body's inherent dignity, or both, are side constraints, preventing desecrations even if these are performed with the best intentions and for the best purposes (discussed in Ali & Maravia, 2020).

If extraction can be permissible, it remains to be asked under what conditions precisely. Questions remain in particular about whose consent is necessary in these cases—Muslims believe that the body belongs to God, but that decision-making about it is delegated, primarily but not exclusively to the person whose body it is – also to their family, and possibly their community, where they cannot decide for themselves (on the role of the family see Chapters 3 and 18) In Fatemeh's case there are two difficult questions in particular: whether her own view on the matter ought to be decisive; and if not, whether her family (in this case, her husband and parents) must be unanimously in favor of donation or merely not unanimously against.

SUGGESTED READINGS

For an excellent review of these and other issues in Islamic bioethics, see
> Sachedina, Abdulaziz Abdulhussein. 2009. *Islamic Biomedical Ethics: Principles and Applications.* Oxford: Oxford University Press.

For discussion of the argument that Islamic law counsels deference to science in determining death, see:
> Miller, Andrew C., Amna Ziad-Miller, and Elamin M. Elamin. 2014. "Brain Death and Islam: The Interface of Religion, Culture, History, Law, and Modern Medicine." *Chest* 146 (4): 1092–101. https://doi.org/10.1378/chest.14-0130.

For a contrasting perspective, insisting that Islam defines death in cardiorespiratory terms:
> Bedir, Ahmet, and Şahin Aksoy. 2011. "Brain Death Revisited: It Is Not "Complete Death" According to Islamic Sources." *Journal of Medical Ethics* 37 (5): 290–4. https://doi.org/10.1136/jme.2010.040238.

For discussion of Islamic opposition to transplantation from corpses, see Sachedina (above) and:
> Ali, M., & Maravia, U. (2020). "Seven Faces of a Fatwa: Organ Transplantation and Islam." *Religions 11* (2): 99. https://doi.org/10.3390/rel11020099

A critical discussion of the "dead donor" rule in the United States:
> Truog, Robert D., and Franklin G. Miller. 2008. "The Dead Donor Rule and Organ Transplantation." *New England Journal of Medicine* 359 (7): 674–5. https://doi.org/10.1056/NEJMp0804474.

For an argument that transplantation is permissible from both living donors and corpses, see:

Chamsi-Pasha, H., & Albar, M. A. (2021). "Do Not Resuscitate, Brain Death, and Organ Transplantation: Islamic Perspectives." *Avicenna Journal of Medicine*, 7 (2): 35–45. https://doi.org/10.4103/2231-0770.203608

A major North America Islamic Council expresses their position, in favor of transplantation, here:

Padela, A. I., & Auda, J. (2020). "The Moral Status of Organ Donation and Transplantation within Islamic Law: The Fiqh Council of North America's Position." *Transplantation Direct*. https://doi.org/10.1097/TXD.0000000000000980.

The study was certainly deeply unethical. But it is important to understand why, and where there may still be some ethical controversy here.

Respect for persons requires respecting their right not to be experimented upon without their free and informed consent. The researchers clearly violated this requirement. To obtain their informed consent the researchers should have, at the very least, told the men that they were in a study, that the study offered no treatment for syphilis, and that the study procedures, including the painful and dangerous spinal taps, did not contribute to their care.

The question of whether the study violated beneficence is, surprisingly, somewhat harder. Beneficence in research does not categorically rule out exposing subjects to interventions whose risks outweigh their potential benefits (i.e., interventions that expose subjects to "net risks"), since the purpose of research is different than the purpose of clinical care. Nor does beneficence categorically rule out inviting subjects to forgo treatment if they are willing to do so. What beneficence does require is that any net risks subjects are willing to accept be counterbalanced by sufficiently large benefits to society (Wendler and Miller 2007).

To be sure: if certain popular depictions of the Tuskegee study were correct in every detail, beneficence would clearly be violated. According to these depictions, untreated syphilis was invariably deadly; when the study began there was already a strong consensus in favor of treating latent syphilis with arsenic-based therapies; arsenical therapy would have been accessible to most subjects outside the trial if the researchers had not prevented them from receiving it; and the study was never even intended to obtain results that would have any public health value but was only conducted to satisfy the curiosity of researchers who suspected that the disease manifested differently in Black people than in White people.

Some scholars have recently challenged the accuracy of these depictions (Benedek and Erlen 1999; White 2000). They do not dispute the violations of informed consent. They also concede that once penicillin became available, the study likely violated beneficence from that point on. But they contend that prior to penicillin the popular depiction exaggerates the study's net risks and underestimates its potential social value.

Whether withholding arsenic-based therapy added to the net risks of the study depends on the appropriate benchmark for comparison. If the baseline is the best treatment available to the participants outside the study, then withholding it would not have contributed to the study's net risks. This is because the men were indigent and funding for free treatment programs had dried up with the Depression, so they would not have received treatment anyway. If instead the baseline is the best treatment the researchers could have provided to their subjects (perhaps given a larger budget than they actually had) then the withholding may have contributed to the study's net risks. The magnitude of those risks would depend on how badly off the men would be without treatment and how much better off they would be with treatment.

Still, beneficence requires that the net risks of the study's nontherapeutic procedures like the spinal tap, together with whatever risks were added by the withholding of treatment, be justified in light of the anticipated social value of the study. According to the scholars who have been challenging the popular depictions of the study, it did have a worthy public health rationale; namely, to establish a no-treatment benchmark against which the effectiveness of new treatments could be compared. Arsenic-based therapies, though partially effective, were expensive, hard to administer, painful, hazardous, and had extremely low completion rates. There was an urgent need for new treatments that were quicker and safer. The Tuskegee study, it was hoped, would provide a reliable benchmark for evaluating future treatments that would be given to Americans, especially Black Americans. (If this is so, then the study may not have been as inconsistent with justice in subject selection as is often assumed, since members of a vulnerable population could have been selected, at least in part, in order to benefit other members of that population.)

That said, this social value was at best aspirational since there were critical defects in the study's design and implementation that kept it from realizing its potential social value. With the advent of penicillin, the net risks of a no-treatment study went radically up and its social value went radically down. At that time, if not before, it should have been obvious that exposing indigent Black men to these net risks was indefensible. Thus, it seems clear, in the end, that the study as a whole remains a paradigm of unethical clinical research.

SUGGESTED READINGS

A study showing that the disclosure of Tuskegee in 1972 not only increased mistrust in the health system among Black men who became aware of it but also appears to have increased their mortality rate:

> Alsan, Marcella, and Marianne Wanamaker. 2017. "Tuskegee and the Health of Black Men." *The Quarterly Journal of Economics* 133 (1): 407–55.

For a comprehensive account of the context and details of the Tuskegee study by a historian of healthcare:

> Reverby, Susan. 2009. *Examining Tuskegee: The Infamous Syphilis Study and Its Legacy.* Amsterdam: Amsterdam University Press.

Description of the study and ethical assessment:

> Jones, James H. 2008. "The Tuskegee Syphilis Experiment." In Ezekiel Emanuel et al. (eds.), *The Oxford Textbook of Clinical Research Ethics* (pp. 86–96). Oxford: Oxford University Press.

An influential ethical framework for research ethics and regulations:

> National Commission. "The Belmont Report." Federal Register, 1979.

For a very plausible, though contested, interpretation of Belmont's beneficence requirement:

> Wendler, D., and F. G. Miller. 2007. "Assessing Research Risks Systematically: The Net Risks Test." *Journal of Medical Ethics* 33 (8): 481–6.

For arguments that some critics of the study have neglected its historical context:

> Benedek, Thomas G., and Jonathon Erlen. 1999. "The Scientific Environment of the Tuskegee Study of Syphilis, 1920–1960." *Perspectives in Biology and Medicine* 43 (1): 1–30.

> White, Robert M. 2000. "Unraveling the Tuskegee Study of Untreated Syphilis." *Archives of Internal Medicine* 160 (5): 585–98.

This book contains a valuable chapter on Tuskegee, as well as chapters on other research that exploited Black Americans both before and after Tuskegee:

> Washington, Harriet. 2006. *Medical Apartheid: The Dark History of Medical Experimentation on Black Americans from Colonial Times to the Present.* New York: Harlem Moon

USING OR MISUSING?
Short-Course AZT Trials

THE CASE

Randomized controlled trials make frequent use of placebos. This becomes controversial when a placebo is given to some subjects *instead* of care that has already been proven effective.

It is sometimes important to learn whether a certain medicine works at all, even if no one expects it to work as well as or better than already proven medicines. Difficult moral issues arise when, in order to answer that question, researchers give the medicine to some people and compare them to other people who are given no medicine at all. These issues arose in a particularly complicated way in a real-world case involving pregnant women with HIV.

Pregnant women who are HIV-positive can transmit HIV to their infants during pregnancy, delivery, and breastfeeding. In 1994 researchers in the United States made a breakthrough discovery; namely, that if pregnant women were given oral doses of the anti-retroviral drug AZT early in pregnancy, an IV-infusion of AZT during delivery, and their infants were given oral doses for six weeks, the transmission rate was reduced from 25 percent to 8 percent. This "long course" immediately became the standard of care in the developed world. However, the standard of care for the prevention of

DOI: 10.4324/9781032640525-37

mother-to-child transmission in the developing world continued to be nothing at all, because the long-course regimen was too expensive ($800) and logistically demanding to be feasible there. In response to this problem the National Institutes of Health encouraged researchers to investigate cheaper and simpler alternatives. A "short course" of AZT was one promising candidate. Unlike the long course, this regimen commenced late in pregnancy, did not require an IV-infusion, and did not give doses to infants, making it cheaper and easier to administer.

Although everyone approved of the goal of investigating the short course, the means by which some researchers chose to investigate it proved to be controversial. Instead of randomly assigning pregnant women to the short course or the long course, these researchers assigned them to either the short course or a placebo. The use of a placebo control meant that dozens of infants whose lives could have been saved by the long course instead became infected and died. The researchers defended the use of a placebo arm on the grounds that it was necessary to settle the question of whether the short course was better than nothing, which was the only relevant question for the developing countries that could not afford the long course. (Historical data from the placebo arms of previous trials would not have provided a reliable benchmark for comparison because there was a great deal of variation in the background rate of transmission in different subject populations (Wendler et al. 2004)).

Although the short-course AZT trials remain controversial, most ethicists think that trials like this can be permissible provided: (a) the subjects give free and informed consent (i.e., they understand that they might receive a placebo); (b) they lack access to that proven care outside the trial; (c) the placebo arm is scientifically necessary to answer a sufficiently important question, and (d) the community hosting the research is treated fairly. In that case, the subjects have nothing to lose from participating and others like them in their community and elsewhere have much to gain (Wendler et al. 2004). Nevertheless, when one of the subjects in these trials was asked how she would feel if she were now to learn she had received placebo, she responded, "I would say quite simply that that is an injustice" (Hawkins 2008). What is there to be said in favor of and against this charge of injustice?

RESPONSES

One way to support the charge of injustice is by claiming that withholding the long course from the subjects in the placebo arm violates a *duty of easy rescue*. The subjects may be no worse off in the trial than outside of it, but on this view the researchers have a positive duty to make them better off by giving them the best available care. It might be argued, however, that this is not really an *easy* rescue, since something of great importance would be sacrificed if the researchers did their best to save the infants from HIV: the knowledge gained from the placebo-controlled trial, which had the potential to save thousands of other infants in the future (Hawkins 2008).

Another possible criticism is that withholding the long course violates a *role-based obligation* belonging to the researchers as physicians. If the subjects are also the researchers' patients, as some claim (Shah 2004), withholding care from those patients to benefit patients in the future would violate their professional obligation to prioritize the patient now in front of them. However, it is not clear that we should posit a physician–patient relationship between researchers and subjects. Even if a clinical researcher is also a physician (and many are not), this does not entail that everyone the physician-researcher interacts with using their medical skills becomes their patient, any more than being a lawyer makes everyone you talk to about the law your client. It may be hard for subjects in a clinical trial to tell whether the researcher is acting as their physician or merely as a researcher, since the interactions and settings are often similar. But that is a reason for researchers to take care to ensure that the subjects understand that the researcher is not their personal physician, not necessarily a reason for researchers to act as if they were the subjects' personal physician.

Even if the subjects are not the researchers' patients, it might still be claimed that researchers have the same duty of loyalty to their subjects that physicians have to their patients. But if this was really what society expected from researchers, then we would also expect researchers to be criticized for each of the numerous ways they routinely depart from providing personalized care to their subjects, such as randomizing treatment and doing biopsies and blood draws for purely research purposes. Researchers are sometimes criticized for not doing enough to ensure subjects understand how research departs from personalized care, but rarely for these departures themselves.

Perhaps the most common way of framing the criticism of the researchers in the short-course trials is that, in using a placebo rather than an active control, the researchers are wrongfully *exploiting* the subjects in the placebo arm. It is true that the researchers are not merely neglecting those subjects: they are using those subjects, since the success of the trial relies on the subjects' cooperation and specifically on infants in the control arm becoming infected at a high enough rate to allow the efficacy of the short course to be assessed.

According to one account, wrongful exploitation occurs whenever one party takes advantage of injustice in the sense that the other party was willing to accept their terms only because they've been unjustly deprived of more attractive opportunities. An example would be getting someone to agree to work as your housekeeper for a below-market wage because, due to their membership in a group that suffers from rampant discrimination in education and employment, they lack better opportunities (Malmqvist 2013). On this account, whether the researchers are exploiting the subjects in the placebo arm (as well as the subjects in the short-course arm) would depend on whether the subjects' lack of access to the long course was due to injustice.

Other ethicists have taken issue with this account, arguing that taking advantage of injustice is neither a necessary nor sufficient condition for exploitation. One influential alternative focuses exclusively on the fairness of the terms of the transaction itself (Wertheimer 2012). According to this view, a transaction is exploitative when one party is receiving less or paying more than would be fair, regardless of whether the terms are accepted because of background injustice. Whether the short-course trials count as exploitative on this view will depend on whether the terms offered to the subjects are fair: a 50 percent chance of receiving short course or placebo (and perhaps some payment and ancillary care) in exchange for their time and for permitting the collection of and use of their data.

It is not entirely clear how to analyze the fairness of this transaction in isolation. But it does, at least, seem to compare favorably to many labor-market transactions that occur in these settings. A woman enrolled in this trial gets monitoring and some care, as well as potential access to a promising medication, in exchange for much less sacrifice of time and effort than she can expect to give up, for much less pay, at most available jobs. If some – certainly not all, but some – of the standard labor-market transactions in these settings are morally acceptable, then this transaction may be too.

SUGGESTED READINGS

Provides an influential framework for evaluating trials in developing countries and uses it to defend the short-course AZT trials and the later placebo-controlled nevirapine trials, the results of which, unlike the AZT trials, did save millions of lives:

> David Wendler, Ezekiel Emanuel, and Reidar Lie, 2004. "The Standard of Care Debate: Can Research in Developing Countries Be both Ethical and Responsive to Those Countries' Health Needs." *American Journal of Public Health* 94 (6): 923–928.

For defenses of placebo-controlled trials against the "duty to rescue" objection:

> Jennifer S. Hawkins, 2008. "Exploitation and Placebo Controls." In Jennifer S. Hawkins and Ezekiel J. Emanuel (eds.), *Exploitation and Developing Countries* (pp. 246–85). Princeton, NJ: Princeton University Press.

> Millum, Joseph, and David Wendler. 2018. "The Duty to Rescue and Randomized Controlled Trials Involving Serious Diseases." *Journal of Moral Philosophy* 15 (3): 298–323.

Chapter 5, "HIV and the Second-Rate Solution," contains a very readable journalistic account of these trials and other similar ones:

> Sonia Shah. 2004. *The Body Hunters.* New York: The New Press.

Offers novel explanation for what makes taking advantage of injustice wrong (when it is wrong):

> Malmqvist, Erik. 2013. "Taking Advantage of Injustice." *Social Theory and Practice* 39 (4): 557–80.

Presents his fair transaction account of exploitation and applies it to international clinical trials:

> Alan Wertheimer, 2012. "The Obligations of Researchers amidst Injustice or Deprivation," In Joseph Millum and Ezekiel J. Emanuel (eds.), *Global Justice and Bioethics* (pp. 279–304). Oxford: Oxford University Press.

WHAT CAN CONSENT JUSTIFY?

Challenge Trials for COVID-19

THE CASE

Consent is almost always necessary for clinical research to be ethical. Is it also sufficient? This question became especially pressing in the heart of the COVID-19 pandemic, when there was an extremely urgent need to develop and test new vaccines.

The standard way to evaluate new investigational vaccines is a field trial. This trial design requires enrolling thousands of subjects, randomly selecting half to receive the vaccine candidate and the other half a placebo, and then waiting for enough infections to occur naturally to determine whether the vaccine candidate protects against infection and/or severe disease. Early in the COVID-19 pandemic, when an effective vaccine was desperately needed, the use of an alternative and more controversial trial design was proposed; namely, a "human challenge trial" or "controlled human infection trial." In this design, as in the field trial, participants are randomized between a vaccine candidate and a placebo. The difference is that in a challenge trial the researchers deliberately expose all subjects to the virus. This design requires far fewer subjects and delivers results very quickly, since there is no need to wait for infections to accumulate naturally. The hope was that the use of this design would accelerate vaccine development, and

DOI: 10.4324/9781032640525-38

in the context of a global pandemic, getting an effective vaccine to the public more quickly had the potential to save many thousands of lives.

Although the idea of infecting healthy people with pathogens may be unsettling, challenge trials are frequently used today to aid in the development of vaccines and therapies for infectious diseases like influenza, cholera, and malaria. If challenge trials are not uncommon, why was the proposal to use this same design to evaluate vaccine candidates for the novel coronavirus especially controversial? The main reason was that, since the early days of extremely dangerous and even deadly challenge trials, a consensus had emerged that challenge trials should only be conducted on diseases that are either self-limiting or that can be cured, so that the risk of permanent harm to the subjects is negligible (Miller and Grady 2001). There is still no cure for COVID-19 and the risk of permanent harm is not negligible, even in young and healthy subjects. Would a challenge trial on COVID-19 have been ethical early in the pandemic or possibly even now when there are several effective vaccines on the market?

RESPONSES

Although everyone concedes the necessity of obtaining valid consent from subjects before deliberately infecting them with a dangerous virus, one common concern is that researchers would not be able to reliably obtain valid consent from COVID-19 challenge trial subjects because their consent could not be adequately informed or, if payment were necessary as an inducement, truly voluntary (Bramble 2020).

The concern about information is that, since knowledge of the long-term effects of the virus was incomplete and estimates of the risks of its effects were highly uncertain, the subjects would be in no position to give "truly informed" consent. In reply, it could be argued that although valid consent requires some minimal understanding of what is being consented to, its validity depends less on the completeness of the information the subjects have and more on whether the researchers have done anything improper in obtaining their consent (O'Neil 2018). If the researchers withheld something they knew from the subjects or misled them, then the subjects' consent would be invalid because it was improperly obtained. But so long as the researchers tell the subjects everything they know, do not mislead, and are open about the gaps in their knowledge then should the subjects decide to consent despite the uncertainty, their consent would still be valid (Keren and Lev 2022).

The concern about voluntariness is that an offer of payment, which might be needed to recruit subjects to participate in a study that exposes them to net risks, would apply too much pressure to consent on low-income subjects. In response, it may be argued that consent is rendered involuntary only by pressure that derives from a threat to violate their rights if they do not consent. An offer of payment, even to someone who has a low income, is not coercive in this way.

Even on the assumption that these trials can reliably obtain valid consent from their subjects, there remain potential objections. One objection is that researchers, who are often also physicians, have a role-based obligation not to impose risks of harm or discomfort on their patient for no medical reason. Yet, although physicians normally have such an obligation to their patients, the role of clinical researcher is not a (directly) helping profession, like physician or nurse, but has the distinct function of producing knowledge that can be used to benefit future patients. Arguably, occupiers of this role are not constrained by an obligation to "do no harm" to their subjects (Brody and Miller 2003).

Although it is generally accepted that researchers may impose *some* net risks on subjects, there is also a general consensus that there is an upper limit to the risks that may be imposed, no matter how important the results. If this consensus is correct, then we would need to determine whether infecting subjects with COVID-19, in the absence of a cure, would exceed this upper limit. This would require both identifying the upper limit (for discussion, see Miller and Joffe 2009) and determining whether challenge trials could be designed in a way that would, even in the absence of a cure, avoid exceeding the cap on risks.

Why believe there is an upper limit on net risks? One possible reason is paternalistic. Consent procedures, no matter how carefully implemented, cannot guarantee that competent subjects giving valid consent are not, unbeknownst to the researchers, making a mistake by their own lights because they secretly harbor overly rosy estimates of the risks or are consenting impulsively. A ceiling on allowable risks would keep relatively poor (though still competent) decision-makers from making very costly mistakes. A different and non-paternalistic rationale for a limit is that the publicization of a very bad outcome could undermine public trust, thereby making it more difficult to recruit future subjects and, in the case of vaccine research, to achieve high vaccination rates.

Even if we assume that the researchers can reliably obtain valid consent and that the net risks can be brought below some absolute cap, many ethicists claim the study results must still have sufficient "social value" to justify those risks. The greater the risks, the greater the social value must be. The most common criticism of COVID-19 challenge trials is that they are unlikely to meaningfully accelerate vaccine development and that therefore the risks to the subjects cannot be justified by the study's social value (Shah et al. 2020). One of the issues is that the selection of only young and healthy subjects, which many believe is required to avoid excessive risks, may also keep it from meaningfully speeding up vaccine development. Since a vaccine that works in that select group may not work in the groups that need a vaccine the most the challenge trial may not be able to replace a field trial after all.

Perhaps challenge trials would still have sufficient social value if they saved time by helping to identify the most promising candidates for further field trials (Eyal 2020). But suppose they didn't—would that mean they were unethical? A trial lacking significant social value would not seem to wrong consenting subjects, so long as the trial was not falsely advertised to them as having important social value. That said, there are at least two other reasons to think such a trial may be unethical. First, when research is publicly funded, its organizers have an obligation to the public to put the public's resources to good use, and a study without any redeeming social value would squander those resources. Secondly, there could also be a reason, pertaining to the ethics of regulating research, for review boards to prohibit studies whose risks seem excessive given the slight value of the value of the information to be gained. Altruistically motivated subjects are willing to make sacrifices for worthy ends, but most subjects lack the expertise necessary to evaluate the social value of a study themselves and researchers may tend to overestimate the significance of their own research. Removing the option of enrolling in a study with insufficient social value would protect altruistic subjects from running risks they would not accept if they were in a better position to assess the value of the study.

SUGGESTED READINGS

Account of the ethical conditions that challenge trials normally must meet:
> Miller, Franklin G., and Christine Grady. 2001. "The Ethical Challenge of Infection-Inducing Challenge Experiments." *Clinical Infectious Diseases* 33 (7): 1028–33.

Criticizes COVID-19 challenge trials on a wide variety of moral grounds but makes an exception under one set of conditions:
> Bramble, Ben. 2020. *Pandemic Ethics: 8 Big Questions of COVID-19.* 1st ed. Bartleby Books.

For a defense of moralized conceptions of the validity conditions for consent to research:
> O'Neil, Collin. 2018. "Consent in Clinical Research." In Andreas Muller and Peter Schaber (eds.), *The Routledge Handbook of the Ethics of Consent* (pp. 297–310). Abingdon: Routledge.

Argues that while incompletely informed consent can be valid, misinformed consent cannot:
> Keren, Arnon, and Ori Lev. 2022. "Informed Consent, Error, and Suspending Ignorance." *Ethical Theory and Moral Practice* 25 (2): 351–68.

Argues that the roles of clinical researcher and personal physician are morally distinct:
> Brody, Howard, and Franklin G. Miller. 2003. "The Clinician-Investigator: Unavoidable but Manageable Tension." *Kennedy Institute of Ethics Journal* 13 (4): 329–46.

For a discussion of upper limits to permissible research risks:
> Miller, F. G., and S. Joffe. 2009. "Limits to Research Risks." *Journal of Medical Ethics* 35, (7): 445–9.

Critique of COVID-19 challenge trials on the grounds of insufficient social value:
> Shah, Seema K., Franklin G. Miller, Thomas C. Darton, Devan Duenas, Claudia Emerson, Holly Fernandez Lynch, Euzebiusz Jamrozik, et al. 2020. "Ethics of Controlled Human Infection to Address COVID-19." *Science* 368 (6493): 832–34.

For a thorough defense of challenge trials against common objections:
> Eyal, Nir. 2020. "Why Challenge Trials of SARS-CoV-2 Vaccines Could Be Ethical Despite Risk of Severe Adverse Events." *Ethics & Human Research* 42 (4): 24–34.

A RIGHT TO TRY?

Access to Experimental Medicines

THE CASE

We celebrate the refusal of the United States Food and Drug Administration (FDA) to approve thalidomide (a drug that turned out to cause severe birth defects) for use outside of clinical trials. But terminally ill patients sometimes seek unproven drugs knowing that they will not be alive by the time the clinical trials evaluating the safety and efficacy of those drugs have been completed. Should the FDA have the right to block or burden their access to those drugs?

Abigail Burroughs was a student at the University of Virginia when she was diagnosed with squamous cell carcinoma of the head and neck in January 2000. After several unsuccessful rounds of chemotherapy and radiation therapy her doctors had run out of FDA-approved options, but they told her there were two experimental drugs being evaluated in clinical trials that might work on her tumor. Abigail did not meet the eligibility requirements for either trial. But the FDA permits terminally ill patients who have exhausted all other treatment options and cannot participate in a trial evaluating the experimental drug to receive it from a drug company willing to provide it, but only if, in the judgment of the FDA, the potential benefits of the drug for the patient outweigh its risks. In this instance both drug companies

DOI: 10.4324/9781032640525-39

were unwilling to provide their experimental drugs to Abigail, as they often are, out of concern about the potential for bad publicity and liability from an adverse outcome. Sadly, Abigail died in June 2001. Five years later one of those drugs was approved by the FDA for her kind of cancer.

Shortly after her death, Abigail's father founded the Abigail Alliance for Better Access to Developmental Drugs, which filed a lawsuit against the FDA arguing that the terminally ill had a constitutional right to receive experimental drugs, so long as they are found to be safe, and the provider is willing. Such a right would limit the FDA's authority to forbid access to experimental drugs as well as its authority to control the price companies can charge the terminally ill. (The FDA did not block Abigail's access and it approves most requests, but the Abigail Alliance believed that more drug companies would be willing to provide their experimental drugs to the terminally ill if the FDA did not cap the prices they can charge.)

Ultimately, the Abigail Alliance's arguments did not prevail at court (*Abigail Alliance v. von Eschenbach* 2007). But if we set aside the specifically legal issues, is there a compelling ethical argument to be made against the FDA's authority to restrict or burden access to experimental drugs?

RESPONSES

One justification for the FDA's authority is that, by restricting patients' menu of drug options to those drugs it has determined to be safe and effective, the FDA can prevent patients from making bad choices. Although the FDA does permit some terminally ill patients to access unproven drugs, it reserves the right, on a case-by-case basis, to block access to drugs it judges to be a bad bet for the patient, as well as to cap the prices companies can charge to prevent them from driving exploitative bargains with desperate patients. This justification can be challenged on the grounds that whether the risks of an unproven drug are worth running for a patient depends on something outside the scope of the FDA's expertise; namely, that patient's attitude towards death. Even price capping is not always in the interests of terminally ill patients since companies might decide not to offer the drug to the patient rather than to offer it at the low price.

Another objection, which would apply even if the FDA did know better than patients what was in their best interests, is that it is objectionably paternalistic to prevent competent adults from making bad self-regarding choices.

There is, however, an alternative non-paternalistic justification for the FDA's authority that is not vulnerable to these objections (Kilbride et al. 2020). That justification is that the FDA's restrictions on access are necessary to secure an important public good, specifically the data that enables patients and their physicians to make evidence-based decisions about drugs. If drug makers were able to sell drugs for a profit without having to first obtain FDA approval they would have little incentive to sponsor long and expensive clinical trials. Even if companies were willing to sponsor some trials for marketing purposes, patients would have little incentive to enroll in them if they could obtain those drugs outside a trial. Although treatment in clinical trials is often free, these trials are also often randomized, which means patients must accept a chance that they won't receive the drug they are seeking and could even, in some trials, receive a placebo.

One objection to this justification is that the costs of the FDA's restrictions outweigh their benefits. These costs include depriving patients of beneficial drugs that would have been developed but for the expense of sponsoring clinical trials to obtain FDA approval ("drug loss") and beneficial drugs that were developed and ultimately approved by the FDA but were unavailable to patients while they were being studied ("drug lag"), such as Abigail Burroughs (Flanigan 2017). Sometimes opponents of the FDA's restrictions argue in addition that those restrictions violate a basic right, either a right to self-medication belonging to all patients, or as the Abigail Alliance argued, a right to medical self-defense belonging only to terminally ill patients.

A right to self-medication is a right that would challenge nearly every restriction on access to drugs. One way to argue for it is as follows (Flanigan 2017). Everyone would agree that Debbie, who prefers to try to manage her diabetes with diet rather than insulin, has a right to refuse insulin treatment, even against medical advice. But, so the argument continues, any reason to believe that Debbie has this right is equally a reason to think that Danny, who prefers to manage his diabetes with insulin or some experimental drug instead of diet, has a right against interference with his access to those drugs. Therefore, since we endorse the right to refuse treatment, we must also endorse a right against interference with access to treatment –that is, a right to self-medication.

While there are some reasons supporting a right of refusal that support a right to non-interference with access as well (e.g., our autonomy interest in deciding for ourselves how we manage our health), there does appear to be at least one justification—arguably the best justification—underpinning a right to refuse that does not also support a right against interference with access. Injecting Debbie with insulin without her consent would violate her right to bodily integrity. But the right to bodily integrity would not imply that Danny has a right against interference with access to drugs, since it is possible to block Danny's access to drugs in ways that do not invade his body, e.g., by preventing the drug maker from selling it to him or pharmacies from dispensing it to him without a prescription (Quong 2020).

A right to medical self-defense, unlike a general right to self-medication, is a right possessed only by the terminally ill against the FDA's effort to block or burden their access to experimental drugs that might help them avert a mortal threat to their lives. One argument for a right to medical self-defense is by analogy with the established right to self-defense (Volokh 2007). We have a right to use force against someone when we reasonably believe this is our only option to stop them from using (illegal) force against us, even when our use of force is unlikely to succeed and might even backfire on us. If we have such a right, how could we not also have a right to defend ourselves against deadly pathogens and cancers by using unproven drugs?

However, the right to self-defense does not include a right to defend ourselves by any means whatsoever. Reasonable regulations on gun ownership for the sake of protecting public health do not infringe the right to self-defense. There is also a public health interest in preserving the incentive to enroll in clinical trials, and restricting access to experimental drugs may be necessary to protect that incentive. It might even be necessary to prevent patients who, like Abigail, are ineligible for clinical trials from receiving them, because it is relatively easy for patients with the help of a cooperative physician to render themselves ineligible for those trials (Menikoff 2008).

SUGGESTED READINGS

Appellate court case that reviewed and rejected the Abigail Alliance's arguments for a constitutional right of the terminally ill to access experimental drugs that have passed a Phase 1 safety trial:

> *Abigail Alliance for Better Access to Developmental Drugs v. von Eschenbach*, 495 F.3d 695 (D.C. Cir. 2007)

Argues that currently far too many drugs require prescriptions:

> Kilbride, Madison, Steven Joffe, and Holly Fernandez Lynch. 2020. "Prescription Requirements and Patient Autonomy: Considering an Over-the-Counter Default." *Hastings Center Report* 50 (6): 15–26.

Argues for a basic right to self-medicate that would challenge nearly all drug regulation, including the prescription requirement:

> Flanigan, Jessica. 2017. *Pharmaceutical Freedom: Why Patients Have a Right to Self-Medicate*. 1st ed. New York: Oxford University Press.

Criticizes the inference from a right to refuse treatment to a right against interference with access to treatment:

> Quong, Jonathan. 2020. "On Flanigan's Pharmaceutical Freedom." *HEC Forum* 34 (3): 257–68.

Argues by analogy with self-defense for a broad right to medication access:

> Volokh, Eugene. 2007. "Medical Self-Defense, Prohibited Experimental Therapies, and Payment for Organs." *Harvard Law Review* 120 (7): 1813–47.

Explains some of the practical issues with allowing access to patients who are ineligible for trials:

> Menikoff, Jerry. 2008. "Beyond Abigail Alliance: The Reality Behind the Right to Get Experimental Drugs." *Kansas Law Review* 56 (5): 1045–74.

PART VIII

FAIR DISTRIBUTION

SUGGESTED READINGS

The classic article and its surprising conclusions:

Taurek, John. 1977. "Should the Numbers Count?" *Philosophy & Public Affairs* 6 (4): 293–316.

Defends the intelligibility and significance of its being impersonally worse that five die than that one dies against Taurek:

Parfit, Derek. 1978. "Innumerate Ethics." *Philosophy & Public Affairs* 7 (4): 285–301.

In Taurek's tradeoff examples we are certain about the outcomes; this article defends an approach to handling more realistic tradeoffs where we only know the risks of certain outcomes:

Frick, Johann. 2015. "Contractualism and Social Risk." *Philosophy & Public Affairs* 43 (3): 175–223.

The original presentation of the balancing approach, which Kamm has developed and defended in subsequent articles:

Kamm, Frances. 1993. *Morality, Mortality, Volume 1: Death and Whom to Save from It* (pp. 101 and 114–19). Oxford: Oxford University Press.

Raises important objections to Kamm's balancing approach (as well as T.M. Scanlon's similar tie-breaking approach):

Otsuka, Michael. 2004. "Skepticism about Saving the Greater Number." *Philosophy & Public Affairs* 32 (4): 413–26.

OURS OR US?

Henrietta Lacks and the HeLa Cell Line

THE CASE

Asking about allocation in bioethics inevitably leads to the question: what is up for grabs? In the case of Henrietta Lack, and her descendants, what was allocated was once a part of her. What difference might that make?

In January of 1951, 31-year old Henrietta Lacks felt a "knot in her womb," and sought treatment at Johns Hopkins Hospital in Baltimore, the only facility in the area that was willing to treat Black patients like her. Less than a hundred years after the end of chattel slavery in the United States, Lacks entered a medical system rife with paternalistic norms that particularly devalued the lives and opinions of Black people. At the hospital, physicians performed a biopsy, and diagnosed cervical cancer. After receiving radiation treatment, Henrietta Lacks died of her disease in on October 4, 1951. But her cells lived on, as researchers at Johns Hopkins discovered that her particular cells were special: they could reproduce indefinitely in culture, where other cells would die out after a certain number of generations. This "HeLA" cell line became foundational to the basic biomedical science of the twentieth century. Though the doctors that performed the initial biopsy did not personally profit from the cell line, careers and fortunes

DOI: 10.4324/9781032640525-42

were made from these cells. But yet, for many years neither Henrietta nor her surviving family were aware that this part of her body had been used in this way. Indeed, ironically, many of her children and descendants have been unable to access the medical advances her cells were so instrumental in helping to produce (Skloot 2011).

RESPONSES

The case of Henrietta Lacks raises several significant problems in bio-ethics. A first set of issues relates to the original clinical encounter. It is not clear whether her physician intended, at the time of biopsy, to use her cells in research. But if he did, Henrietta was not informed of this. It might be argued that this would mean her physicians did not have her full and valid consent to the biopsy itself, as a clinical procedure. Others might maintain that, given prevailing medical norms at the time, she should have expected that her cells once removed might be used for any purpose whatsoever. Others still might argue that she does not need to know everything about the procedure to validly consent to it: since the use of the tissues in research did not affect her interests, information about this use did not need to be disclosed.

These arguments thus also raise a broader set of issues concerning what sorts of interests patients like Henrietta Lacks have in their separated cells. Some of these relate to other technological advances that have occurred in the interim. For instance, the advent of genome sequencing raises problems of privacy with stored biosamples. These problems can sometimes be addressed by "de-identifying" or "anonymizing" stored samples. But in the near future, it may become difficult or impossible to ensure that stored cells cannot be re-associated with their source. For this reason and others, few would deny that present-day diversion of clinical samples to research purposes requires informed consent (though there is some controversy about whether consent is required for each individual research study; see Grady et al. 2015 for discussion).

Much more controversial is the question of whether patients like Lacks have an intrinsic interest in what happens to their cells—most prominently, whether patients *own* their separated tissues in a way that gives them a right to control what happens to them or a right to share in any profits they help to produce. The case of John Moore, similar in some respects to Lacks's, is interesting here (for discussion see Lavoie 2016). Moore like Lacks agreed to clinical biopsies; like Lacks's tissues, Moore's were used for socially beneficial, and profitable, research. Moore, unlike Lacks, found out and sued, under a legal theory that presumed that he *owned* these tissues and therefore was entitled to a share of the profits from their non-consensual use. The Supreme Court of California disagreed, arguing that if anyone owned these tissues it was the scientists, since it was they who would use them in research likely to produce public benefit.

Bioethicists have been divided over whether the court was correct to deny ownership rights here. Some argue that, at least in cases (like Lacks's) where there are no additional costs or burdens to contributing tissue to research, patients have done nothing to earn a property claim in their separated tissues (Truog et al. 2012). Moreover, putting a price on human tissue raises long-standing concerns about the commodification of the human body and distortions of the clinical relationship. Others think that that these concerns are overblown, and that allowing tissues to be used to benefit others is a contribution in itself, deserving of some return (Johnson and Wendler 2015).

Part of the reason Lacks's case has received so much attention in recent years is that it raises social issues broader than questions about the precise content of consent to clinical biopsies or the best legal regime for controlling rights over tissues. Henrietta Lacks was Black, and so are her descendants. Some bioethicists take this background of injustice as a kind of narrative context for the issues considered above—"added poignancy," as two well-known ethicists put it (Faden and Powers 2011). One might well argue that there are even deeper connections between the ethics of consent, policies around tissue ownership, and issues of racial and social justice.

So, for instance: consider the relevance of Lacks's social position to the claim that she implicitly consented to the use of her tissues in research. Among the factors that can undermine validity of consent are the unjust absence of alternative options, and the failure to provide information that might be relevant to a person's choices, given their values. Lacks, a Black woman in the segregated city of Baltimore, had little choice but to seek care at Hopkins, a research institution, since other facilities in the area would not accept Black patients. In that sense, she seems to have been forced, by social conditions and the absence of a choice to opt out, into participation in research. And Black people in America have and had ample reason to distrust medical research institutions (see Washington 2006; Chapters 29, 36)— suggesting that, if Lacks had been explicitly asked to contribute to research, she might have had reason to refrain, or at least ask for something substantial for her family in return.

Nor ought we, necessarily, to regard the plight of some of Henrietta Lacks's family members as mere emotional color, largely irrelevant to the core ethical issues about what happened to her and her tissues. In a better world, a world where everyone can expect to share in the benefits of medical progress, people can perhaps be asked to contribute tissues to research without specific recompense. But this duty to contribute becomes much less plausible when imposed on patients from communities with substantially less and less secure access to the benefits of new medical knowledge.

That said, concerns about social justice may also press against specific compensation. Many would argue that anyone without adequate access to healthcare is the victim of the same sort of injustice, whether their parent or grandparent contributed tissues to research or not. To this way of thinking, talk of compensation for tissue donors moves us away from central concerns of social justice in healthcare, which require provision of adequate healthcare to everyone (Faden and Powers 2011).

SUGGESTED READINGS

The now-classic account of Henrietta Lacks and her cells is:
> Skloot, Rebecca. 2011. *The Immortal Life of Henrietta Lacks*. New York: Broadway Paperbacks.

On the somewhat similar Moore case:
> Lavoie, Jennifer. 2016. "Ownership of Human Tissue: Life after Moore v. Regents of the University." *Virginia Law Review* 75 (7): 1363–96. http://www.jstor.org/stable/1073130.

For an argument that clinical samples can be used for research without compensation:
> Truog, Robert D., Aaron S. Kesselheim, and Steven Joffe. 2012. "Paying Patients for Their Tissue: The Legacy of Henrietta Lacks." *Science* 337 (6090): 37–8. https://doi.org/10.1126/science.1216888.

Responding, in favor of compensation, on grounds that "donation" is actually an important form of cooperative contribution:

Johnson, Rebecca A., and David Wendler. 2015. "Challenging the Sanctity of Donorism: Patient Tissue Providers as Payment-Worthy Contributors." *Kennedy Institute of Ethics Journal* 25 (3): 291–333. https://doi.org/10.1353/ken.2015.0021.

On what sort of consent is required for sample research, irrespective of compensation, see:

Grady, Christine, Lisa Eckstein, Ben Berkman, Dan Brock, Robert Cook-Deegan, Stephanie M. Fullerton, Hank Greely, et al. 2015. "Broad Consent for Research with Biological Samples: Workshop Conclusions." *The American Journal of Bioethics* 15 (9): 34–42. https://doi.org/10.1080/15265161.2015.1062162.

For some discussion of the importance of social justice issues for interpreting this case in particular:

Faden, Ruth, and Madison Powers. 2011. "A Social Justice Framework for Health and Science Policy." *Cambridge Quarterly of Healthcare Ethics* 20 (4): 596–604. https://doi.org/10.1017/S0963180111000338.

And finally, for broader context around the use of Black subjects in medical research:

Washington, Harriett. 2006. *Medical Apartheid*. New York: Harlem Moon.

35

ALLOCATION IN AN EMERGENCY
Ventilator Triage

THE CASE

Nothing raises the moral stakes of an allocation decision like a shortage of lifesaving resources. During the COVID-19 pandemic we have witnessed shortages in personal protective equipment, tests, therapeutics, and vaccines. Early on there was concern that shortages in intensive care unit (ICU) beds, ventilators, and extracorporeal membrane oxygenation (ECMO) machines would force physicians to turn away some dying patients and healthcare institutions rushed to put rationing protocols in place. In the United States hospitals did not run short of ventilators, as had happened in Italy, but patients did die for lack of access to ECMO (Fink 2021). Rationing protocols are used to rank patients in order of priority for a resource they all need but cannot all be given. How should the following three patients be ranked, each of whom will die without mechanical ventilation? (See White and Lo 2021 for a similar rationing problem.)

Patient A: 25-year-old woman with cystic fibrosis. Her predicted hospital mortality (the chance that she will die before leaving the hospital even if she gets on a ventilator) is 50 percent. Her life expectancy should she survive the acute illness is another 20 years, to age 45.

DOI: 10.4324/9781032640525-43

Patient B: 65-year-old female with no comorbidities. Her predicted hospital mortality is 60 percent. Her life expectancy should she survive is another 20 years, to age 85.

Patient C: 65-year-old male with incurable metastatic cancer. His predicted hospital mortality is 70 percent. His life expectancy should he survive is one year, to age 66.

RESPONSES

One natural proposal for prioritizing is that scarce health resources should be distributed in whatever way would yield the greatest (health-related) benefits (Singer 2009). To implement this proposal, we need a way to measure benefits. One obvious benefit that ventilators offer is the saving of a patient's life. To maximize the expected lives saved with scarce ventilators, we would prioritize patients with the lowest predicted hospital mortality, resulting in this ranking: A, B, C.

However, if the lives of either of two patients could be saved, but one would go on to live another 50 years and the other only ten, there is a clear sense in which the first patient gets a larger benefit from the resource. Measuring expected benefits in terms of life years rather than lives saved captures this difference in the size of the benefits. If we assume for simplicity the same predicted hospital mortality for A, B, and C, then the ranking in terms of life years saved would be: A & B, C.

Life years is still an incomplete measure of health-related benefits since a hip replacement can benefit a patient by improving the quality of their life without increasing its quantity. A popular unit for comparing the size of benefits in terms of both quantity and quality of life is the quality-adjusted life year (QALY), where a life year spent in perfect health is 1 QALY and a life year spent with a condition that detracts from health-related quality of life is somewhere between 0 and 1, depending on its severity. For example, if the health-related quality of life with arthritic hips is .6 and with hip replacement is .8, then a patient who is expected to live 20 more years either way will gain $20(.8) - 20(.6) = 4$ QALYs. QALYs can also be used to measure the benefits of life-extending treatments. Notice that a patient with a comorbidity that reduces their health-related quality of life may gain fewer QALYs from ventilation than a patient who is otherwise healthy even if they would gain the same number of life years. On the assumption that cystic fibrosis detracts significantly from health-related quality of life, then the ranking by QALYs might plausibly be: B, A, C.

Although published guidelines all take lives saved into account, far fewer consider life years and hardly any consider quality of life. This is in part because rationing protocols based on life years and QALYs disadvantage social groups with lower life expectancies, such as Blacks, Hispanics, and the disabled, exacerbating already existing inequalities in health (Mello et al. 2020, and see Chapters 12 and 37).

But there is also an influential individualistic objection to any rationing scheme based entirely on maximizing benefits, however they are measured; namely, that it neglects fairness. When two patients would benefit the same amount, everyone would agree that the tie should be broken by random selection, if only to protect against the influence of favoritism or prejudice. But sometimes, even when one patient would benefit more than another, random selection remains appealing. For example, if each of two dying COVID-19 patients would gain 20 life years from ventilation, but one would gain fewer QALYs because of arthritis or even something more serious like paraplegia, many would still prefer selecting between them randomly rather than giving the ventilator to the patient who would benefit more. Why? Although one patient would benefit more, they still seem to have equally strong claims to the resource, since they need it just as much, and fairness requires equal treatment for equally strong claims (Broome 1984).

Or so it seems. Some would argue that even when both patients would be dead without a ventilator, one patient might still need it more and so have a stronger claim. The needier person in this way of thinking is the one who will have had the least (good) life without the resource (Kamm 1993). Consider Patient A, the dying 25-year-old who with ventilation will survive until 45, and Patient B, the 65-year-old who will survive until 85. Each will be equally badly off without the ventilator from now on since each will be dead. But it is the 25-year-old who will have had the least life if they die now. If the 65-year-old dies now, they will have enjoyed 65 years of life, which is more life than the 25-year-old would enjoy even if they were given the ventilator.

Most ethicists are pluralists about rationing (Emanuel 2020). Although fairness is very important, benefits matter too, and sometimes it may be more important to be cost-effective than to be fair, especially when one patient would have only a very remote chance of benefiting from the resource and another would have a very high chance of benefiting. There are other things allocation might take into account as well. Some have argued that patients who made a choice not to be vaccinated have weaker claims to scarce resources than vaccinated patients, because they are partially responsible for their need. Some ethicists have advocated taking socioeconomic status into account (White and Lo 2021). There are also some that have advocated making race a factor on the grounds that, after controlling for age, Blacks and Hispanics have experienced a higher death rate from COVID-19 than Whites—an inequality that is traceable to unjust structural factors or structural racism (Schmidt et al. 2021). Some argue for including race just because it is a proxy for as yet unknown extra-risk factors, which would make it relevant to degree of need. The more controversial position is that, even among individuals who are similar in terms of need and benefit, some priority should still be given to Black or Hispanic patients on the grounds that the application of such a policy would help to prevent the pandemic from widening already existing unjust inequalities in health between racial and ethnic groups.

SUGGESTED READINGS

For the story about the ECMO (extracorporeal membrane oxygenation) shortage in New York:

> Fink, Sheri. 2021. "The Rationing of a Last-Resort Covid Treatment." *The New York Times*, August 12.

White and Lo produced one of the most fully worked out and influential rationing protocols during the pandemic, which assigned points on the basis of both medical and socioeconomic factors:

> White, Douglas B., and Bernard Lo. 2021. "Mitigating Inequities and Saving Lives with ICU Triage during the COVID-19 Pandemic." *American Journal of Respiratory and Critical Care Medicine* 203 (3): 287–95.

Advocates for maximizing QALYs as the principle of rationing:

> Singer, Peter. 2009. "Why We Must Ration Health Care." *The New York Times*, July 17.

For why rationing based on expected life years or QALYs would disadvantage marginalized groups:

> Mello, Michelle M., Govind Persad, and Douglas B. White. 2020. "Respecting Disability Rights – Toward Improved Crisis Standards of Care." *New England Journal of Medicine* 383 (5): e26.

Develops the idea of comparative fairness to justify the use of random selection in rationing:

Broome, John. 1984. "Selecting People Randomly." *Ethics* 95 (1): 38–55.

Develops sophisticated approach to rationing, distinguishes different conceptions of need, among other things:

Kamm, Frances. 1993. *Morality, Mortality: Volume I: Death and Whom to Save from It.* New York: Oxford University Press.

Important pluralistic framework for rationing in the pandemic:

Emanuel, Ezekiel J., Govind Persad, Ross Upshur, Beatriz Thome, Michael Parker, Aaron Glickman, Cathy Zhang, Connor Boyle, Maxwell Smith, and James P. Phillips. 2020. "Fair Allocation of Scarce Medical Resources in the Time of Covid-19." *New England Journal of Medicine* 382 (21): 2049–55.

Discusses the interaction of race and pandemics historically and today:

Matose, Takunda A., and Paul C. Taylor. 2022. "Pandemics and Race." In Michael Boylan (ed.), *Ethical Public Policy within Pandemics* (pp. 95–115). Cham: Springer Nature.

Explains how common rationing protocols disadvantage Black patients and recommends fixes:

Schmidt, Harald, Dorothy E. Roberts, and Nwamaka D. Eneanya. 2021. "Rationing, Racism and Justice: Advancing the Debate around 'Colourblind' COVID-19 Ventilator Allocation." *Journal of Medical Ethics* 48 (2): 126–30.

Please add one more reference at the bottom:

For an account of the moral significance of waiting time:

John, Tyler M., and Joseph Millum. 2020. "First Come, First Served?" *Ethics* 130 (2): 179–207.

36

DATA AND DISTRIBUTION
Algorithmic Fairness

THE CASE

In the twenty-first century healthcare decisions are increasingly guided by predictions generated by machine-learning algorithms. Consider the following real-world example (Obermeyer et al. 2019):

Patients who suffer from multiple chronic illnesses often develop serious complications that land them in the emergency room (ER) and require costly hospitalization. Placing the patients who are at the highest risk of developing complications in a program that provides extra monitoring and care can help to prevent those complications, benefiting patients and reducing costs. Since these high-risk management programs are expensive, selecting the right patients is crucial. Many health systems rely on an algorithm to help them predict which patients will be the sickest in the following year so that they can be enrolled in one of these programs.

Machine-learning algorithms like the one used by these health systems learn to make predictions about the future from "training data" about the past. The training data for this algorithm consisted of information about previous patients such as their age, sex, diagnoses, and medications in a particular year, together with the amount of money that was spent on their care in the following year. This meant that

DOI: 10.4324/9781032640525-44

the algorithm was learning to predict costs, not health needs. But it is common to use costs as a proxy for needs because costs, unlike health status, can be reduced to a single variable and costs are strongly correlated with needs. The algorithm then generated risk scores for patients based on their characteristics, and all patients with scores above a certain cutoff were automatically enrolled in the program.

A group of outside researchers were given access to this algorithm to assess its performance. The algorithm did a good job in general of predicting how sick patients would be the following year. But when the researchers compared its performance for Black and White patients, they discovered something troubling. Among patients with the same risk scores, the algorithm significantly underestimated future illness for Black patients. For example, when they looked at patients who had received scores above the cutoff for automatic enrollment, Black patients had on average 4.8 chronic conditions the following year and White patients only 3.8.

Black patients and White patients who had been assigned the same risk scores did end up with similar healthcare costs the following year, which is what the algorithm had been trained to predict. So what went wrong? It turned out to be the reliance on costs as a proxy for needs that gave rise to the disparity. The reason that the risk scores underestimated the health needs of Black patients relative to White patients is that less money is spent on healthcare for Black patients than for equally sick White patients. Part of the reason for this is that Black patients have lower incomes on average, and it is harder for lower-income patients to obtain healthcare because they are more likely to lack means of transportation, spare time, and relevant knowledge. The other part of the explanation relates more directly to racial identity, e.g., Black people are less trusting of healthcare because of historical abuses (see Chapters 29 and 34), and there is evidence that doctors recommend less care for Black patients than for White patients (Hoffman 2016).

As a result of having been trained on costs rather than health needs, the algorithm's scores systematically underpredicted the future health needs of Black patients relative to White patients. This meant that very sick Black patients were less likely to be enrolled in the program than equally sick White patients. Even worse, it was the very fact that Black patients had been underserved in the past that led to these Black patients being underserved in the present.

RESPONSES

As this case reveals, algorithms can lead to biased decisions. But it is important not to lose sight of their advantages over unaided human decision-making. Disparities in health between different racial groups are largely attributable to the unjust distribution of the social determinants of health, but there is a body of research showing that Black patients are also disadvantaged at the point of care. Some providers may provide lower quality of care to Black patients on purpose, but more often the provision of lower-quality care is the result of cognitive biases. For example, physicians may base a decision on a mistaken belief that there is an association between race and some clinically relevant factor when there is no association. More commonly, they may believe an association is stronger than it is; for example, they may believe that most Black patients have a certain risk factor when it is only the case that Black patients are more likely to have it than non-Black patients. Mistakes like these can lead to under- and over-treatment of Black patients, and since these biases tend to be shared by other providers, they also contribute to disparities in health between racial groups (Wasserman 2011).

Machine-learning algorithms can help decision-makers avoid such mistakes. These algorithms do need to be given a large set of accurate and representative examples to learn from, which they do not always receive. But if the data they are given are good, the algorithms' predictions will not rely on race when it is not associated with the outcome of interest, and when it is associated with the outcome, the predictions will not give race any more weight than it deserves.

Even when human decision-makers rely on accurate generalizations, they are prone to another failing that machine-learning algorithms can help them to avoid. When decision-makers rely on statistics about someone's group, they are sometimes accused of having failed to treat that person *as an individual*, even when the statistics are reliable. Ethicists have offered differing accounts of what exactly is required to treat someone as an individual rather than merely as a member of some group (Lippert-Rasmussen 2011; Wasserman 2011). But they are united in the view that it does not demand avoiding reliance on generalizations entirely. Rather, the right to be treated as an individual is violated when the decision-maker relies on a generalization

increasingly concerned with these issues, as societies in the West attempt to do better in reckoning with racial injustice. Ethicists in particular have the expertise to ask two sorts of questions about these cases. They can ask: how is Rachel wronged, here? And they can ask: what would count as doing better? (Leaving it to patient groups, policy experts, and physicians, how exactly to produce better care for patients like Rachel.)

RESPONSES

The fundamental problem Rachel faces, of course, is an inability to get good care. This is clearly unjust, in her case, but we can ask: why?

One answer is simple. Rachel has a right, perhaps a human right, to adequate healthcare (Hassoun 2016), and John's actions, coupled with social structures that make better care difficult or impossible to access, prevents her from enjoying that right. This may (or may not) be an important part of the moral story here, but it is not the whole story. Human rights to health and healthcare are controversial, given that it is not feasible to keep everyone in full health, and the difficulty of defining what counts as adequate healthcare. And someone who does not believe in a right to healthcare might still think that Rachel was wronged here. Even assuming there is a general right to adequate care, it seems that there are other rights at stake here too: particularly rights against *discrimination*, which John violates. That is to say, even if we think it is bad, wrong, or unjust for anyone to lack adequate care, we might think it is worse, another wrong, or more unjust if that lack is explained by racial and/or gender identification.

Another obvious injustice in this case relates to how John himself treats Rachel: he doesn't listen to her, and the reason he doesn't listen is his perception of her identity as a member of a racialized group. This involves both explicit bias, based in beliefs he is aware of and would endorse on request, and implicit bias, subconscious attitudes or habits of judgment which he may not be aware of but which nonetheless affect his practice. His concern that she is drug-seeking reflects endorsement of a belief that Black patients presenting for pain are substantially more likely to be drug addicts. He may also share the belief, shockingly widespread among medical professionals, that Black people have significant physiological differences relevant to pain perception (Hoffman et al. 2016).

It is also possible that John holds one or both of these attitudes *implicitly*, acting as if he believed them even if he would not in fact endorse them if asked. As described, it seems likely he has other implicit biases in any case: say, biases that lead him to take Rachel's pain testimony specifically less seriously because of her gender (Fitzgerald and Hurst 2017). Similar biases generalized may explain why he has been insensitive to mounting evidence that uterine fibroids are a serious and treatable condition, rather than "benign and harmless."

The result of these biases together is an instance of what philosopher Miranda Fricker famously called *testimonial injustice*, where someone's credibility is unfairly denied or delimited, often because of prejudice or stereotypes about people like them (discussed in Kidd and Carel 2017). Doctors cannot effectively treat their patients if they do not listen; if they do not listen because of unjust bias, then the resulting lack of effective treatment is a consequence of injustice and perhaps therefore a further injustice in itself.

These testimonial injustices can have additional effects, effects which further undermine the ability of patients like Rachel to get good care in the future. If the medical system tends to devalue the testimony of a given category of patients, medical knowledge is likely to have major gaps with respect to those patients. Recognized conditions may be underdiagnosed; some conditions, like chronic fatigue syndrome, or long COVID, may not have been recognized at all. This undermines the ability of physicians to give good care to patients, but it also undermines the ability of patients to understand what is going on in their own lives and bodies, resulting in what has come to be called interpretive or *hermeneutical* injustice.

A medical system characterized by these forms of injustice is a place where some people are not listened to, or understood, as well as others. In addition to directly undermining the provision of good care, these testimonial and hermeneutic injustices may also make it less likely that those treated unjustly will access what care is available. Why would you trust a medical establishment that treats you like that—particularly if that establishment has a history of treating people like you much worse (see, for instance, Chapter 29, on the Tuskegee experiment; or Chapter 34, on Henrietta Lacks)? There is good evidence that distrust of medicine reduces use of medical services in African Americans (Benkert et al. 2019). To the extent that this distrust is caused by the medical system itself, it represents an important structural barrier to access to care, and an important issue for bioethics in itself (Newman 2022).

That brings us to structural injustice more generally (Powers and Faden 2019). Rachel's disastrous outcome was a result not only of having a bad doctor but of having poor access to alternative care. That could be explained in part by understandable distrust of the system. But it may also have other structural causes. If Rachel is, like many Black people, economically disadvantaged, she may have difficulty finding physicians that will accept public health insurance or affording deductibles on her low-cost private plan. It is possible that she is sick in the first place because she lives in a less healthy environment, with more exposure to pollution. Non-medical racial discrimination may also play a role, even if she is affluent: producing psychic stress which can have serious somatic effects. It is easy enough to see that all of these barriers are unjust. But understanding why they are unjust, a more difficult task, can help us to see what it would mean to adequately recognize and respond to injustices like those Rachel faces, as she tries to access adequate medical care.

SUGGESTED READINGS

We owe the inspiration for this fictionalized case to a real-world example detailed in:
>   Wiggleton-Little, Jada (2022). Presentation in Panel "How Should We Think and Talk about Pain?" Georgetown University, Washington, DC.
Discussing and defending a human right to health and healthcare:
>   Hassoun, N. (2015). "The Human Right to Health." *Philosophy Compass*, *10*(4): 275–83. https://doi.org/10.1111/phc3.12215
For empirical reviews of data on implicit bias in healthcare professionals, see:
>   FitzGerald, C., & Hurst, S. (2017). "Implicit Bias in Healthcare Professionals: A Systematic Review." *BMC Medical Ethics*, *18*(1): 19. https://doi.org/10.1186/s12910-017-0179-8

>   Vela, M. B., Erondu, A. I., Smith, N. A., Peek, M. E., Woodruff, J. N., & Chin, M. H. (2022). "Eliminating Explicit and Implicit Biases in Health Care: Evidence and Research Needs." *Annual Review of Public Health 43*: 477–501. https://doi.org/10.1146/annurev-publhealth

For a review of racial disparities in pain assessment:

Hoffman, K. M., Trawalter, S., Axt, J. R., and Oliver, M. N. (2016). "Racial Bias in Pain Assessment and Treatment Recommendations, and False Beliefs about Biological Differences between Blacks and Whites." *Proceedings of the National Academy of Sciences of the United States of America 113* (16), 4296–301. https://doi.org/10.107

On testimony and epistemic injustice in healthcare, in particular:

Kidd, I. J., & Carel, H. (2017). "Epistemic Injustice and Illness." *Journal of Applied Philosophy 34* (2): 172–90. https://doi.org/10.1111/japp.121723/pnas.1516047113

For a comprehensive discussion of research on medical mistrust:

Ramona Benkert, Adolfo Cuevas, Hayley S. Thompson, Emily Dove-Medows, and Donulae Knuckles (2019). "Ubiquitous Yet Unclear: A Systematic Review of Medical Mistrus." *Behavioral Medicine 45* (2): 86–101. https://doi.org/10.1080/08964289.2019.1588220

And the relevance of medical mistrust (and untrustworthiness), and the discourse around it, to bioethics:

Newman, Alyssa M. 2022. "Moving beyond Mistrust: Centering Institutional Change by Decentering the White Analytical Lens." *Bioethics 36* (3): 267–73. https://doi.org/https://doi.org/10.1111/bioe.12992.

Finally, on structural injustice, with particular attention to healthcare contexts:

Powers, Madison, and Ruth Faden. 2019. *Structural Injustice: Power, Advantage, and Human Rights*. Oxford: Oxford University Press.

providers like Dr. Park to limit the scope of their practice for reasons of conscience (Ancell and Sinnott-Armstrong 2017). In response it could be argued that if shoulder surgeries were becoming very hard for patients to obtain, it might not be unfair to require orthopedists to offer shoulder surgeries as a condition for licensing. Another issue is that, even if we think providers should have the leeway to turn away potential patients requesting a service they find it tedious or time-consuming to perform, we might think they would need a much better reason for denying that service to someone who is already their patient.

The next two arguments attempt to explain why reasons of conscience are more worthy of accommodation than reasons of mere personal preference. According to one view, CRs should be accommodated to protect professionals' interest in moral integrity—an interest in leading a life in accord with their deepest moral convictions (Brock 2008). Although it is always possible for a provider to preserve their integrity by quitting their job, the thought is that a professional should not have to pay a steep price to protect this important interest. Ethicists who cite moral integrity as the reason for accommodation usually restrict the eligible CRs to those that are sincere, empirically informed, based on a core not peripheral moral conviction, and (much more controversially) reasonable in some sense (Little and Lyerly 2013). Importantly, preserving one's moral integrity may require a provider to refuse to make a referral as well. If Dr. Park refuses to perform elective abortions because she thinks abortion is murder, then since providing a referral would be to help arrange someone's murder, this would presumably bother her conscience too.

A different kind of reason for accommodation is based on the interests of the public. There are already shortages in certain specialties like ob/gyn and refusing to accommodate CRs would exacerbate those shortages by causing people to leave or avoid those specialties. Accommodating CRs might also help the profession to make moral progress. Medicine has needed moral reform in the past (e.g., forced sterilizations), and the thought is that it is more likely to achieve whatever moral reforms are necessary now or in the future if, by accommodating CRs, it keeps its critics inside the profession (Kim and Ferguson 2022).

Ethicists who have considered these arguments and weighed up these interests have arrived at different conclusions. There are three basic positions. One position is that CRs should almost never be accommodated (Rhodes 2019). Another is that, except in emergencies, CRs should almost always be accommodated, including CRs to make referrals. The most popular position, however, is a position that lies between these two extremes, known as the "conventional compromise" (Brock 2008). According to this position, since the profession has been granted a monopoly on providing medical services, it has a collective obligation to ensure that the full range of services are accessible to patients. But there are different ways the profession can distribute individual obligations to providers that would be consistent with its meeting this collective commitment, and according to the conventional compromise position, one way is better than the others. That way is, roughly, to permit providers to conscientiously refuse to provide a service to a patient, but only if they make a referral to someone who is willing to provide that service for the patient. Under this compromise, services will be kept accessible to patients, although they will still be vulnerable to the sting of moral disapproval, like Dr. Park's patient. Providers won't be required to provide services they regard as immoral, but will be required to be complicit, from their point of view, in the provision of that service by someone else.

Turning at last to the urologists' refusal to treat sexual dysfunction in previous sex offenders, this is a refusal to treat a type of patient. Even ethicists who think Dr. Park's refusal should be accommodated tend to take a dim view of refusals targeting types of patients. Few ethicists would, for example, be in favor of accommodating a provider who refused to provide intrauterine insemination to lesbians. Treating lesbians less favorably than other patients is wrongful discrimination. Is what the urologists are proposing wrongful discrimination? On the one hand, they are not denying treatment to the men because they believe they don't deserve healthcare. It is only because treating their sexual dysfunction would pose a risk to others. Since it seems appropriate to refuse to hire someone with a history of sex offending to work in a day care, precisely because hiring such a person poses a risk to children, then it seems like it should also be appropriate to refuse to treat these men. On the other hand, we tend to think that doctors are supposed to focus exclusively on the medical needs of their patients and ignore whatever bad things addressing those needs might enable or encourage the patient to do. We may be free to consider risks in making a hiring decision that doctors are not and should not be free to consider in deciding whether to treat someone (Douglas 2016).

SUGGESTED READINGS

First-hand account of the experience of having one's request for an elective abortion rejected on moral grounds:
>Dye, Leslie Kendall. 2017. "My Gynecologist Wouldn't Give Me an Elective Abortion—So I Broke Up With Her." Self.Com. https://www.self.com/story/gynecologist-elective-abortion

Douglas was asked to advise the urologists and this article resulted from that consultation:
>Douglas, Thomas. 2016. "Refusing to Treat Sexual Dysfunction in Sex Offenders." *Cambridge Quarterly of Healthcare Ethics* 26 (1): 143–58.

Develops an influential version of the conventional compromise:
>Brock, Dan W. 2008. "Conscientious Refusal by Physicians and Pharmacists: Who Is Obligated to Do What, and Why?" *Theoretical Medicine and Bioethics* 29 (3): 187–200.

Some argue that it is only refusals that target types of patients that are impermissible:
>Ancell, Aaron, and Walter Sinnott-Armstrong. 2017. "How to Allow Conscientious Objection in Medicine While Protecting Patient Rights." *Cambridge Quarterly of Healthcare Ethics* 26 (1): 120–31.

For a compromise approach to conscientious refusals in reproductive medicine:
>Little, Margaret, and Anne Drapkin Lyerly. 2013. "The Limits of Conscientious Refusal: A Duty to Ensure Access." *Virtual Mentor* 15 (3): 257–62.

Argues that the best reason for accommodation is to ensure that the profession continues to make moral progress:
>Kim, Eric J., and Kyle Ferguson. 2022. "Conscientious Objection, the Nature of Medicine, and the Need for Reformability." *Bioethics* 36 (1): 63–70.

Argues against accommodating most refusals, on the grounds that refusals normally violate physicians' professional obligations:
>McLeod, Carolyn. *Conscience in Reproductive Health Care: Prioritizing Patient Interests.* Oxford: Oxford University Press, 2020.

>Rhodes, Rosamond. 2019. "Conscience, Conscientious Objections, and Medicine." *Theoretical Medicine and Bioethics* 40 (6): 487–506.

STAY AT HOME?
The Ethics of Lockdowns

THE CASE

Public health ethics has long grappled with justifying impositions on freedom, like quarantines or mandatory vaccines (Chapter 41). These raise long-standing ethical questions about what some can be forced to do to protect others. Still, ethical answers were not ready to hand when these issues became more important than ever, at the beginning of the COVID-19 pandemic.

On March 20, 2020, New York State instituted a "stay at home" order, barring people from leaving their homes except for certain reasons. At that time, SARS-COV2, a novel and highly infectious respiratory virus, was spreading rampantly: likely tens of thousands were infected, and hundreds had already died. Other states and jurisdictions also imposed lockdowns. The state of Hawaii announced a stay-at-home order on March 22; at the time, there were only 50 confirmed cases. Some counties, and countries, imposed highly restrictive measures before any cases were confirmed at all. At the same time, the virus was spreading at an unknown, but rapid, rate, and it was not yet known just how dangerous the associated COVID-19 disease was. Hospitals had been partially overwhelmed by critically ill patients in Italy and

DOI: 10.4324/9781032640525-48

FREEDOM AND VIRUSES
The Case of Medical Misinformation

THE CASE

Public health, we might think, is mainly about the spread of disease. But how diseases spread depends on what people do, and what people do depends on what they believe.

The spread of medical misinformation has surely made the COVID-19 pandemic worse than it might have been. In a crisis people are desperate for information and exposure to falsehoods can impair their decision-making. They may reject proven treatments; may pursue unproven and dangerous treatments; may fail to take standard precautions against infection and transmission; and most importantly, may refuse vaccination. Furthermore, if they discover that someone has misled them, it becomes harder for them to trust other people who are telling them the truth.

Throughout the pandemic social media has been a major conduit for misinformation. There is normally no vetting before someone can post medically relevant content on social media sites, and the more novel and engaging the content (a poor indicator of its accuracy), the more likely it will be shared and promoted by the platform's algorithms. Indeed, false content spreads faster and farther than true content across all categories of information, likely because

DOI: 10.4324/9781032640525-49

the truth tends to be less exciting and more mundane (Vosoughi et al. 2018). It is difficult to estimate the extent to which misinformation has reduced vaccine uptake, but according to one study, exposure to misinformation reduced willingness to be vaccinated by 6 percent (Loomba et al. 2021), a small effect per person but potentially a very large one in the aggregate.

Here are a few of the examples of medical misinformation that have led to calls for tech companies to crack down on it. In 2020, very early in the pandemic, the documentary *Plandemic* was posted on YouTube and Facebook. It featured an interview with the discredited scientist Judy Mikovits who claimed, among other things, that the pandemic had been planned by the elites and that facemasks activate the virus. By the time it was removed a few days later it already had over 8 million views (Frenkel et al. 2020). In early 2022 a group of doctors, in an open letter, called out Joe Rogan for giving conspiracy theorists a platform on his popular podcast and urged Spotify, the company hosting the podcast, to suppress this misinformation going forward. In late 2022 the documentary *Died Suddenly* was released, exposing millions to its claims that vaccines cause people to "die suddenly" from blood clots and also cause cancer, miscarriages, and still births.

Medical misinformation is dangerous, to be sure. But we also value freedom of speech. Is it more important to prevent harm from misinformation or to protect freedom of speech?

RESPONSES

The First Amendment only limits the government's power to restrict speech, not companies that provide public forums like Twitter or Facebook. But if freedom of speech is valuable then we should also be concerned about the power of social media platforms to restrict speech, and also the power of social stigma to silence unpopular points of view (Mill 1859). Since the rationale for removing *Plandemic* and *Died Suddenly* from sites is based on their content and the consequences that might flow from that content, these removals are clear cases of *censorship*. Freedom of speech is normally opposed to censorship, but perhaps there are good reasons for treating medical misinformation as an exception.

One possible reason is that, unlike speech that merely offends its audience, medical misinformation costs lives. However, those who value freedom of speech do not generally regard the potential for harm as a sufficient justification for censorship.

If a video of police brutality is released, we might expect it to provoke a violent reaction. Similarly, disclosing that the mRNA vaccines have the rare but serious side effect of myocarditis no doubt led some people to overreact and decide against vaccination even though the risk/benefit ratio remained overwhelmingly favorable. Yet in neither of these cases would we regard the harms expected to result from this information as an adequate reason for suppressing it.

The difference, of course, is that the harms from the video and the disclosure of the risk of myocarditis are harms caused by the truth—i.e., by information, not misinformation. Still, it may not be immediately clear why we would want to remedy this problem with censorship when we can simply combat falsehood with the truth. Unfortunately, the truth does not always prevail in the contest. We tend to believe what we are told, even if we are at the very same time provided with strong evidence that what we are told is false. As mentioned earlier, on social media falsehoods travel faster and farther than truths. And the posts we are exposed to by our social networks and by the website's algorithms tend to have content that confirms what we already believe, since this keeps us more engaged (Sunstein 2021).

Since medical misinformation is harmful, false, and its effects cannot be neutralized by counter-speech, there is a strong prima facie case for censoring it. But there may also be reasons not to censor false speech. One obvious reason is potential speakers' interest in expressing their thoughts. Preventing someone from saying what they genuinely believe to others is a serious infringement of their liberty to speak their mind (Shiffrin 2016).

Note that this reason only applies if the misinformation is sincerely believed but mistaken. If the speaker disbelieves or does not believe the content but wants to communicate it anyway in order to influence others this is not an interest that deserves much if any consideration at all.

Perhaps surprisingly, there may also be good reasons to think that censorship of misinformation could, in some ways, also be contrary to our interests as an *audience* for speech, not just as potential speakers.

First, if the government or tech companies are given the power to suppress false speech, it is likely they will misuse that power. They may lack the expertise to reliably distinguish the truth from the false and decide to err on the side of caution, depriving us of important truths (Mill 1859). Another reason is that they will be unable to avoid the temptation to use this power to suppress legitimate criticisms of their policies, as has happened in many countries during the pandemic (Human Rights Watch 2021). Perhaps having questions of truth or falsehood settled by an independent tribunal of scientists and requiring a very high standard of proof before it can classify something as misinformation would go some way towards mitigating these problems (Sunstein 2021).

Second, attaching penalties to false speech tends to deter or "chill" valuable true speech. It is one thing to think what you're saying is true and another to be certain enough that it is true and that you could prove its truth to the satisfaction of a court that you would be willing to risk a penalty if it should turn out to be false. Since speakers often don't have much to gain from sharing what they know, it wouldn't take much to deter them from speaking. However, it's not clear this concern applies to censorship by tech companies, which only remove content without penalizing the speaker. And even if false speech was penalized, the chilling effect could be minimized if sincere false speech was protected (i.e., believing what you said), since even if we cannot be sure that what we believe is correct, we can be sure we believe it.

Third, censoring medical misinformation can be counterproductive by making the target a free-speech martyr and attracting more attention to their views (Friedersdorf 2022).

Fourth, John Stuart Mill famously argued that even an audience that already believes the truth on some matter may still have something to gain from exposure to expressions of false opinions. We can only come to *know* the truth, as distinct from merely believing it, when we have considered not only the best reasons in favor of our belief but also the best reasons against it and determined that the reasons in favor are stronger (Mill 1859; Shah 2021). To make such a determination, we need access to the best reasons against our belief, presented in their strongest form, and that requires permitting people who hold the opposite belief to express it and defend it. Mill anticipates the objection that so long as *someone* has weighed up the reasons against the view, we can just come to know it on their authority without having evaluated the reasons against it ourselves. This was the arrangement in the Catholic Church at one point, where the priesthood was permitted access to heretical opinions but not the laypeople. But Mill thinks believing it on this basis alone does not confer genuine understanding or knowledge.

However, it is worth asking whether, when it comes to matters of science, it is advisable for laypeople to "do their own research" rather than simply deferring to the experts, since we may be more likely to end up believing something false than deepening our understanding of the truth.

SUGGESTED READINGS

Evidence that falsehoods travel farther and faster than the truth:
> Vosoughi, Soroush, Deb Roy, and Sinan Aral. 2018. "The Spread of True and False News Online." *Science* 359 (6380): 1146–51.

One attempt to estimate the effect of misinformation on vaccine hesitancy:
> Loomba, Sahil, Alexandre de Figueiredo, Simon J. Piatek, Kristen de Graaf, and Heidi J. Larson. 2021. "Measuring the Impact of COVID-19 Vaccine Misinformation on Vaccination Intent in the UK and USA." *Nature Human Behaviour* 5 (3): 337–48.

Detailed account of how one example of misinformation spread:
> Frenkel, Sheera, Ben Decker, and Davey Alba. 2020. "How the 'Plandemic' Movie and Its Falsehoods Spread Widely Online." *The New York Times*, May 20.

As part of his celebrated case for freedom of speech, Mill argues that audiences have an interest in exposure to false statements of opinion:
> Mill, John Stuart. 1859 (2017). *On Liberty.* Edited by Jonathan Bennett.
> https://www.earlymoderntexts.com/assets/pdfs/mill1859_1.pdf

Chapters 5 and 6 argue that Mill's defense of freedom of speech should not be extended to all false statements of fact:
> Sunstein, Cass R. 2021. *Liars.* New York: Oxford University Press.

Comprehensive philosophical treatment of the ethics and law of false statements:
> Shiffrin, Seana Valentine. 2016. *Speech Matters: On Lying, Morality, and the Law.* Amsterdam: Amsterdam University Press.

Collection of examples of government abuse of medical misinformation laws and regulations:
> Human Rights Watch. 2021. "Covid-19 Triggers Wave of Free Speech Abuse," March 29.

https://www.hrw.org/news/2021/02/11/covid-19-triggers-wave-free-speech-abuse

Argues that restricting medical misinformation does more harm than good:

Friedersdorf, Conor. 2022. "What's the Harm in Medical Misinformation?" *The Atlantic*, February 11.

Presents a compelling interpretation of one of Mill's arguments for free speech that most commentators have dismissed as implausible:

Shah, Nishi. 2021. "Why Academic Freedom Matters." *The Raven*. https://ravenmagazine.org/magazine/why-academic-freedom-matters/

they restrict some freedoms (to decide what medicines are put in our body) in order to protect others (to move about the world free from fear of a potentially deadly or disabling disease).

All that said, for mandates to be justified they actually do have to prevent harm or produce benefit (Copp and Dworkin 2020). To produce the largest benefit, "herd immunity" or disease eradication, mandates have to motivate a large portion of the population to comply. To do more good than harm, putting a mandate in place has to increase vaccination rates sufficiently to outweigh harms and costs of enforcement. In contexts of political polarization, this is hardly guaranteed; in the US, mandates appear to have discouraged some from getting vaccinated, and may have motivated few people who would not have chosen to do so anyway. The jury is out, then, as to whether mandates are justifiable empirically, even if they could be justified ethically.

SUGGESTED READINGS

On the harms of non-vaccination, arguing that even libertarians should accept a case for mandatory vaccination:

Flanigan, Jessica. 2014. "A Defense of Compulsory Vaccination." *HEC Forum* 26 (5): 5–25. https://doi.org/10.1007/s10730-013-9221-5.

A response to Flanigan, agreeing in general but arguing that vaccination requirements depend specifically on judgments about collective harm:

Brennan, Jason. 2018. "A Libertarian Case for Mandatory Vaccination." *Journal of Medical Ethics* 44 (1), 37–43. https://doi.org/10.1136/medethics-2016-103486

Detailing arguments that non-vaccination is an unfair form of "free-riding" on the efforts of other to get vaccinated, see:

Hoven, Mariëtte van den. 2012. "Why One Should Do One's Bit: Thinking about Free Riding in the Context of Public Health Ethics." *Public Health Ethics* 5 (2): 154–60. https://doi.org/10.1093/phe/phs023.

For the idea that requiring people to be vaccinated is relevantly similar to requiring to pay taxes:

Giubilini, A. 2020. "An Argument for Compulsory Vaccination: The Taxation Analogy." *Journal of Applied Philosophy* 37 (3), 446–66. https://doi.org/10.1111/japp.12400

An argument in favor of placing much higher demands on the health of some to protect others:

Fabre, Cecile. 2006. *Whose Body is it Anyway?* Oxford: Oxford University Press.

For discussion of the relation of vaccine mandates in children to parental authority:
Diekema, Douglas S. 2011. "Revisiting the Best Interest Standard: Uses and Misuses." *Journal of Clinical Ethics* 22 (2): 128–33. https://doi.org/10.1086/jce201122204.

A good general review of issues around vaccine mandates, including ethical arguments in favor, and empirical concerns against:
Copp, D., and Dworkin, G. 2020. "Ought We Compel People To Be Vaccinated?" 3 Quarks Daily. https://3quarksdaily.com/3quarksdaily/2020/08/ought-we-compel-people-to-be-vaccinated.html

For an influential statement of the idea that government mandates are only appropriate for protecting others from us, not protecting us from ourselves, see:
Mill, John Stuart. 1859. *On Liberty*. 1st ed. London: J.W. Parker and Son.

Others might say that physicians should not offer this service because treating homosexuality as a suitable object of medical intervention wrongly regards it as a disease, in the process insulting and endangering people who have no desire to change orientation (for discussion see Earp and Vierra 2018). However, this argument seems to presuppose that treating disorders or diseases is all doctors can legitimately do. But this is not at all clear; there are many medical procedures which do not obviously or unproblematically treat disease, but which seem to be sometimes permissible—from contraception and abortion, to elective cosmetic surgery, to psychiatric treatment for ordinary non-pathological life problems like marital difficulties or bereavement and grief (Little 1998; Wakefield 2015).

A second set of questions concerns not what any individual should do in case safe and effective reorientation techniques were available, but rather whether we should allow or encourage these techniques to be developed in the first place. Some ethicists have argued that we should be very wary of developing these technologies in advance of further global progress on acceptance of non-hetero orientations (Aas & Delmas 2018). Premature development of effective and individually safe technologies might be harmful to members of sexual minorities who choose not to use the technology. The idea that people do not and cannot "choose" their orientation has been an important political argument for toleration. Introducing the possibility of "choosing" heterosexuality may imperil the political viability of this argument. It might also introduce pressure on particular members of sexual minority communities to "convert," since they can no longer respond that this is simply not possible for them. And to the extent that, in some places at least, many people take this option, sexual minority communities might be depopulated, depriving remaining members and the world of valuable forms of political solidarity and cultural expression. These harms may, or may not, be significant enough to give medical researchers reasons not to develop technologies, or to give research regulators reasons to discourage, defund, or even ban this research.

A third, related set of questions broadens the lens from the Yeshiva Student case itself to more general issues about changing or choosing orientation, particularly where the change is not in the same "direction." Proponents of developing sexual reorientation technologies have pointed out that they would not always or even primarily be used to "turn gay people straight." Some, motivated by feminist political convictions, might use it as a way to escape the patriarchal meanings and expectations involved in sexual and romantic relationships between women and men (Earp and Vieraa 2018). Others might have personal or ethical reasons to want to "expand their romantic circle," so that they could pursue a broader range or relationships than their existing dispositions to sexual and romantic attraction allow (Thau 2020). Arguably, these uses of this hypothetical technology are less concerning than the use imagined in the Yeshiva case—they do not, for instance, have the same risk of depopulating queer communities, or exacerbating unjust pressures to conform to heterosexual norms.

SUGGESTED READINGS

For the original Yeshiva Student case, see:

> Earp, Brian D., Anders Sandberg, and Julian Savulescu. 2014. "Brave New Love: The Threat of High-Tech 'Conversion' Therapy and the Bio-Oppression of Sexual Minorities." *AJOB Neuroscience* 5 (1): 4–12. https://doi.org/10.1080/21507740.2013.863242.

On the (un)safety and (in)efficacy of current methods for changing sexual orientation:

> American Psychological Association. 2009. Report of the Task Force on Appropriate Therapeutic Responses to Sexual Orientation. Washington, DC: American Psychological Association. www.apa.org/pi/lgbc/publications/.

Arguing that sexual orientation ought not be changed because it is a central feature of the self:

> Nussbaum, Martha C. 2002. "Millean Liberty and Sexual Orientation: A Discussion of Edward Stein's 'The Mismeasure of Desire.'" *Law and Philosophy* 21 (3): 317–34. http://www.jstor.org/stable/3505208.

Two (qualified) defenses of the use of medical techniques for purpose and goals other than the promotion and protection of health:

> Little, Margaret. 1998. "Cosmetic Surgery, Suspect Norms, and the Ethics of Complicity." In E. Parens (ed.), *Enhancing Human Traits: Ethical and Social Implications* (pp. 162–77). Washington, DC: Georgetown University Press.

> Wakefield, Jerome. 2015. "Psychological Justice: Dsm-5, False Positive Diagnosis, and Fair Equality of Opportunity." *Public Affairs Quarterly* 29 (1): 33–76.

For concerns about the harms of even safe and effective reorientation on LGBTQ communities and individuals, see:

> Delmas, Candice, and Sean Aas. 2018. "Sexual Reorientation in Ideal and Non-Ideal Theory." *Journal of Political Philosophy* 26 (4): 463–85. https://doi.org/10.1111/jopp.12159.

by boosting our self-control. But also, if we have a hard time getting ourselves to behave with as much kindness towards other as people as we believe we ought to, an MN that made us more empathetic could help with that. Similarly, if we value nonviolence but have difficulty resisting our aggressive impulses, an MN that reduced our aggression would make that easier for us as well (Pugh 2017).

However, on some views, free will requires more than just the exercise of an ability to act in accord with one's values. It also requires that those values, as well as other mental states on the road to action, be authentically our own (Pugh 2017). For example, when the God Machine intervenes to prevent someone from choosing the wrong, so that they subsequently choose the right, we are not inclined to regard that person as having freely willed the right. Nor would we regard that choice as really theirs if the way the God Machine caused the person to choose the right was by modifying their feelings or values well before they made the choice.

There are a couple things that could be said in reply. First, we've been discussing nonconsensual MNs, but if someone were to consent to these nonrational influences on their motivations, or even simply would not regard those influences as alienating upon reflection (DeGrazia 2014, perhaps the resulting motivations would still be authentic. Secondly, there may be some examples of influences that are unmediated by our rational capacities that do not strike us as diminishing our freedom, such as painting the walls of a prison green to reduce aggression. This is an environmental influence that works via perception, rather than having a direct pharmacological or electrical effect on the brain, but in neither case is the influence mediated by our rational capacities (Douglas 2018). Yet, we might think, acting under these sorts of influences is consistent with free will and moral responsibility. If so, then it may be that we can be good, responsible people—people who choose freely and well—even if it takes some technological intervention to get us there.

SUGGESTED READINGS

The God Machine is from:
> Savulescu, Julian, and Ingmar Persson. 2012. "Moral Enhancement, Freedom, and the God Machine." *Monist* 95 (3): 399–421.

Against the significance of whether an intervention directly targets the brain:

Focquaert, Farah, and Maartje Schermer. 2015. "Moral Enhancement: Do Means Matter Morally?" *Neuroethics* 8 (2): 139–51.

Argues that the "freedom to fall" is necessary for moral responsibility and is extremely valuable:

Harris, John. 2010. "Moral Enhancement and Freedom." *Bioethics* 25 (2): 102–11.

Source of the so-called "Frankfurt cases" that challenge the view that the power to have chosen otherwise is necessary for moral responsibility:

Frankfurt, Harry G. 1969. "Alternate Possibilities and Moral Responsibility." *The Journal of Philosophy* 66 (23): 829–39.

Discusses how different conceptions of free will bear on the question of whether moral enhancements would diminish our freedom:

Pugh, Jonathan. 2017. "Moral Bio-Enhancement, Freedom, Value and the Parity Principle." *Topoi* 38 (1): 73–86.

Argues that moral neuroenhancements do not necessarily threaten our freedom:

DeGrazia, David. 2014. "Moral Enhancement, Freedom, and What We (Should) Value in Moral Behaviour." *Journal of Medical Ethics* 40 (6): 361–8.

Argues that if we regard certain environmental influences on our motivations that are unmediated by our rational capacities as acceptable, then there is no good reason not to accept neural influences like SSRIs and brain stimulation as well:

Douglas, Thomas. 2018. "Neural and Environmental Modulation of Motivation: What's the Moral Difference?" In Thomas Douglas and David Birks (eds.), *Treatment for Crime* (pp. 208–23). Oxford: Oxford University Press.

PART XI

MEDICINE ACROSS BORDERS
Dilemmas of Complicity and Compromise

DOES IT HARM TO HELP?
Rescuing Migrants

THE CASE

Providing medical help to struggling people can have unexpected, and controversial, effects. The migration route that crosses the Mediterranean Sea from Libya to Italy is one of the deadliest migration routes to Europe. In recent years hundreds of thousands of migrants and refugees fleeing extreme poverty, war, and persecution in their home countries have paid smugglers to transport them to Libya, where they wait for months until they are eventually packed into flimsy rubber or wooden boats without life jackets, food, water, or a satellite phone. Often the boat is stocked with just enough cans of fuel to enable it to reach international waters, where the smuggler gets out and returns to Libya in a fast boat, leaving the migrants adrift. Unless they are rescued their chances of surviving are slim. Thousands die in the sea each year. The European Union (EU) used to fund a major rescue operation but stopped because it wanted to limit the flow of migrants. For the past several years the EU has been training, paying, and equipping the Libyan Coast Guard to intercept these boats and return the migrants and refugees to detention centers in Libya—a fate that many of the migrants regard as nearly as bad as death. Many suffer from horrifying

DOI: 10.4324/9781032640525-55

human rights abuses while in detention and often must pay a bribe to be released (Ou 2021).

Since the EU stopped rescuing these boats, several nongovernmental organizations (NGOs) have stepped in to rescue the migrants adrift at sea before their boats sink or capsize. Unlike the Libyan Coast Guard, the NGOs' rescue ships never return the migrants to Libya but instead take them to Italy or other EU ports which are legally obliged to let the migrants disembark and apply for asylum (although they often try their best to deny permission to disembark).

Italy and the EU resent the NGOs' efforts, primarily because they claim that the NGOs' rescue operations increase the number of migrants and refugees who reach the EU's shores. But they also make a moral criticism: that although the NGOs' rescue operations appear to do nothing but good, they also function as an unintended but deadly "pull factor" that incentivizes more migrants to attempt the dangerous crossing by increasing their likelihood of success.

RESPONSE

In response to this criticism, the NGOs argue that there is no evidence that their rescue operations have served as a significant pull factor (MSF 2017). The extreme poverty, human rights abuses, and other potent push factors that are impelling them to leave their home countries and Libya are such powerful motivators that even a substantial reduction in the chances of a successful crossing would be unlikely to discourage migrants from making the attempt. These claims appear to be supported by the data (Cusumano and Villa 2019).

Nevertheless, to draw out some challenging moral questions, let's suppose for the sake of argument that the rescue operations are a significant pull factor and that terminating them would significantly decrease the number of people attempting the dangerous crossing. In that case would the NGOs be morally required to terminate their rescue operations?

Here is one reason to think the answer is no. Even if these rescue operations did have large incentive effects, it wouldn't follow that the operation leads to more fatalities overall, because the operations have another effect—they also reduce the mortality rate of migrants attempting the crossing. This reduction in the mortality rate might more than compensate for the greater number of attempts and, if so, the rescue operations would result in fewer fatalities overall.

In reply, the opponent of these rescue operations might argue that, even if these operations do result in fewer deaths overall, this fact is still not enough to justify them because these operations are *causing* the deaths of the migrants they have incentivized to attempt the crossing and who subsequently die in the attempt. Non-consequentialists believe that while it may be permissible to let one person die to save a greater number, it is normally wrong to kill one person to save a greater number.

However, even if the incentives created by the rescue operations do cause the deaths of some migrants, at least in the sense that the migrants who died would not have made the attempt to cross were it not for those rescue operations, it seems doubtful that the incentives count as *killing* those migrants in any morally relevant sense. Consider the installation of seat belts in cars. The addition of seat belts made a potentially deadly activity safer though still not completely safe. As a result, there must have been some people who were previously too afraid to drive but became willing to drive after seat belts made driving safer. No doubt some of these people did later die in car accidents. Even though they would not have died if seat belts had not been installed in cars, it seems implausible to regard the seat-belt installers as having killed them in any morally significant sense. And this seems analogous to the way that rescue operations bring about deaths.

Some go even further: arguing that it would be *wrong* to stop the rescues, even if they did cost more lives overall. As one human rights expert put it: "To bank on the rise in the number of dead migrants to act as deterrence for future migrants and asylum seekers is appalling. It's like saying, let them die because this is a good deterrence" (UN Human Rights Office 2014). While it may be permissible to let someone die to save a greater number when their death is merely an inevitable side effect of saving the greater number, it is normally wrong to let someone die to save a greater number when their death is the *means* of saving the greater number. Arguably, if you let a boat sink because this is "good deterrence," the victims' deaths are the means by which you deter future crossings. If this reasoning is correct, then even if the rescue operations exerted a pull factor that resulted in more deaths than they prevented, it would be wrong to cease those operations in order to deter migrants from attempting the crossing. (See Chapters 16 and 23 for more discussion of the moral significance of intentions.)

That said, this argument does have several limitations. First, even if this reasoning is correct, it would only disallow ceasing rescue operations for the sake of deterrence. It would still permit ceasing rescue operations for other reasons that don't involve using the deaths that result as a means to some further end. Secondly, the doctrine that it is harder to justify letting someone die as a means than as a merely foreseen side effect is itself highly controversial in ethics. Thirdly, even those ethicists who believe that it can make a moral difference that a death is intended typically also think that it makes far less of a difference when the presence of victim whose death is intended is viewed as an *obstacle* to the achievement of some goal rather than as an *opportunity* to achieve it (Quinn 1989). To illustrate, suppose that to discourage attempted crossings the EU makes a public announcement that it will no longer rescue imperiled boats. Perhaps this announcement would not be perceived as credible unless the EU backs up its words with (in)action by allowing some boats to sink. In that case the presence of the imperiled boats presents the EU with an opportunity it needs to achieve its goal of deterrence. But suppose instead that the announcement is generally perceived as credible on its own, but the EU recognizes that if it were to subsequently rescue some imperiled boats, this would undermine that credibility. In this case the presence of the imperiled boats presents a potential threat to the goal of deterrence, rather than a means of achieving it, and letting the boats sink to protect the credibility of the announcement might be regarded as more defensible.

SUGGESTED READINGS

The director of this documentary was on board a Médecins Sans Frontières (MSF) ship as it rescued several migrant boats, clashed with the Libyan Coast Guard, and tried to find an EU port willing to allow the migrants to disembark and seek asylum:

Ou, Ed, dir. 2021. *Get Away from the Target: On Board a Refugee Rescue Ship Racing for Europe*. https://www.theguardian.com/global/video/2021/dec/02/unsafe-passage-onboard-a-refugee-rescue-ship-racing-for-europe-video photographer or to advance communicative goals of their own. For example, when identifiability carries risks, as it does for survivors of sexual violence, a choice to reveal one's face can display courage and express defiance of local norms that prescribe shame.

To successfully waive a right to privacy, the subject's consent must be adequately informed. Norms for how much information must be disclosed when consent is sought vary with the activity, but in the context of humanitarian photography, unlike photojournalism with adversarial subjects, extensive disclosure is required about how the photo might be used and any risks. Even when subjects are told that once an image is online it is impossible to reel it back in, they may fail to fully appreciate that fact if they are immature, unfamiliar with the online world, or distracted by recent trauma.

In the case of adults, their free and informed consent is normally regarded as enough to make it permissible to take and publish an identifiable photo. It may even be objectionably paternalistic for a photographer to refuse to use a subject's face because they regard their judgment about what risks are worth running as superior to the subject's own judgment. The case of minors is more complicated. Images of suffering children can be especially powerful because of their innocence, but the younger a child is, the less capable they are of appreciating the potential implications for their lives.

There may not be a one-size-fits-all standard. Consider a photo of an orphan taken for the purpose of attracting a sponsor for that very child. Since the child stands to benefit directly and substantially, it would be hard to justify refusing to use the child's face just because there is no adult that can consent on their behalf. Most humanitarian photography, however, primarily benefits third parties, not the subjects themselves, although if they are old enough it may advance their expressive interests.

When there are no serious risks from the publication of such an image and the minor is relatively mature or is young enough that they won't resemble their current self in a few years, then arguably parental consent should only be required if they have parents. When there are serious risks, as in the case of the 16-year-old survivor of rape, then to permit an identifiable photo is to permit that minor to make a sacrifice on behalf of others, and we may be reluctant to permit minors to make substantial sacrifices for others, even for important causes and even with parental consent.

SUGGESTED READINGS

The photo essay in question:

Tavakolian, Newsha, and Sara Kazamiminesh. 2022. "Ituri, A Glimmer Through the Crack." Medécins Sans Frontières.

Tavakolian's response:

Seymour, Tom. 2022. "Magnum Photographer Defends Images of Teenage Gang Rape Victim after Humanitarian Organisation Removes Them from Website." *The Art Newspaper – International Art News and Events.*

Useful discussion of the complicated issues surrounding humanitarian photography, including issues not discussed here, such as respecting the dignity of the subject:

Calain, Philippe. 2013. "Ethics and Images of Suffering Bodies in Humanitarian Medicine." *Social Science & Medicine* 98: 278–85.

Argues that persuasion by images can count as rational persuasion, although images can also, like any other way of presenting information, have distorting effects:

McGrath, Sarah. 2011. "Normative Ethics, Conversion, and Pictures as Tools of Moral Persuasion." In Mark Timmons (ed.), *Oxford Studies in Normative Ethics*, vol. 1 (pp. 268–94). New York: Oxford University Press.

Seminal article on poverty porn:

Lissner, Jorgen. 1981. "Merchants of Misery." *New Internationalist.* https://newint.org/features/1981/06/01/merchants-of-misery

Develops the view that the point of privacy rights is to protect our interest in controlling how we present ourselves to others:

Marmor, Andrei. 2015. "What Is the Right to Privacy?" *Philosophy & Public Affairs* 43 (1): 3–26.

physicians may be helping to sustain the practice of caning in at least two ways. One way is by making it safer, since injurious or disfiguring caning would diminish public support for the practice. The other is by legitimizing caning by producing the appearance that caning is endorsed by a trusted profession.

A physician will exhibit a high degree of complicity on the motivational dimension if they are playing their role *because* this is what the state wants them to do or because they will be helping to sustain the practice. But it would be possible for physicians to act only out of concern for prisoners' health and to do their part *despite* the fact that it assists the state and helps to sustain the practice. We would expect physicians whose motives were genuinely pure in this sense to speak out against the practice to dispel the appearance of endorsement, and to be ready to participate in an effective physician boycott of the practice (i.e., one that would result in the ending of the practice rather than its continuation without any medical supervision) if one were to be organized.

Finally, complicity can be justified, all things considered, so long as the justifying reason is compelling enough to outweigh the moral reason against it, the strength of which will vary with the degree of complicity. Protecting the health of the prisoners may seem like a compelling justification until we recall that, because lashings will be replaced by extra time in prison, the physicians will in some cases be protecting a prisoner's health against their will and perhaps against their overall best interests. This makes the permissibility of physicians' complicity in caning difficult to assess.

SUGGESTED READINGS

Appellate court decision upholding the constitutionality of caning, which contains a detailed description of the practice and defends it against moral objections:

> *Yong Vui Kong v Public Prosecutor* [2015] SGCA 11

Doctors in Singapore defend the practice and their participation in it from criticism by the American Medical Association (AMA):

> UPI. 1994. "Singapore Doctors Support Caning." UPI Archives.

An account of the internal morality of medicine:

> Miller, Franklin G., Howard Brody, and Kevin C. Chung. 2000. "Cosmetic Surgery and the Internal Morality of Medicine." *Cambridge Quarterly of Healthcare Ethics* 9 (3): 353–64.

Describes the job of mixed martial arts (MMA) doctors:

> Whang, Oliver. 2022. "The M.M.A. Doctor's Dilemma: To Stop or Not to Stop the Fight." *The New York Times*, August 8.

Argues for the position that physician complicity in torture can sometimes be justified:

> Lepora, Chiara, and Joseph Millum. 2011. "The Tortured Patient: A Medical Dilemma." *Hastings Center Report* 41 (3): 38–47.

A comprehensive treatment of the morality of complicity:

> Lepora, Chiara and Robert E. Goodin. 2013. *On Complicity and Compromise.* Oxford: Oxford University Press.

DOING THE BEST WITH WHAT WE HAVE?

Foreign Medicine and the Haiti Earthquake

THE CASE

Physicians operating across borders sometimes have to make judgments about whether differences in the resources available to patients should make a difference to care. This issue arose sharply in the aftermath of the 2010 earthquake in Haiti, which killed or injured more than half a million people and left up to two million homeless (Arnaouti et al. 2022). Well-meaning foreign physicians formed teams to bring supplies and provide treatments during short-term stays, often of just a week or two.

Many injuries involved crushed limbs, from falling rubble or being trapped in a collapsed building. When a limb is crushed, there is often a difficult decision to be made about whether it can be salvaged. Compared to amputation, limb-sparing surgeries are more difficult and often require many more total procedures, over weeks or months, to be successful. Orthopedic surgeons from abroad were often not in a position to provide this follow-up care themselves. Concerned about whether follow-up surgeries would be available, some foreign physicians – especially those who had the shortest stays in country – erred on the side of amputation, apparently in hopes of achieving a more definitive resolution before the patient left their care.

DOI: 10.4324/9781032640525-59

The difficulty is that most patients prefer limb reconstruction to amputation (de Lauche et al. 2013). Amputation may be a shorter procedure, but recovery is often more difficult, involving longer hospital stays and higher rates of complications. Disabled amputees in Haiti as elsewhere face stigma and discrimination, and in low-resource setting like Haiti they may find it more difficult to acquire, learn to use, and maintain assistive technologies like prostheses. Indeed after the 2010 earthquake, rates of satisfaction with amputation were low, and further surgeries were in fact needed in roughly 30 percent of cases (Mathuina and Schreeb, 2015).

RESPONSES

These amputations caused a scandal at the time, bringing attention to the fraught ethical issues of "disaster tourism," where foreign volunteers flood a disaster zone, generally meaning well but sometimes doing significant harm in addition to good (Van Hoving et al. 2010). Beyond the scandal, the case raises at least three important issues in the ethics of humanitarian medical assistance. Physicians themselves may not be living up to their ethical and professional obligations, operating against an unfamiliar background of deprivation and inconsistent availability of health services. NGOs organizing care may not bear ultimately responsibility for resource gaps in these contexts, but they have obligations to cope responsibly with the situation they find themselves in. Finally, the underlying injustices that provide the necessary context for this case are ethical issues too, and it is not really possible to understand the interpersonal ethical issues without understanding the structural ones.

Haiti itself is a very poor country, with a per capita income in 2010 of about $1100; barely more than 2 percent of the average income in the US that year. This poverty is no accident: Haiti came into being as a result of a successful revolt against French colonial slave masters. Even after independence, however, the country's economic growth was hobbled by war debt—some of it owed to French themselves, and much to the United States. The US has had a complicated relationship with Haiti, often meddling for its own interests (including the interests of Haiti's US creditors), and sometimes, at least putatively, for the good of Haiti and Haitians themselves. The Haitian health system right if they, and others, have thought about these sorts of clinical, ethical, and political questions in advance of appearing on the scene in the first place.

SUGGESTED READINGS

For a particularly spirited critique of medical "disaster" tourism, in the aftermath of the 2010 earthquake, see:

Van Hoving, Daniël J., Lee A. Wallis, Fathima Docrat, and Shaheem de Vries. 2010. "Haiti Disaster Tourism — A Medical Shame." *Prehospital and Disaster Medicine* 25 (3): 201–2. https://doi.org/10.1017/S1049023X00008001.

For a more measured, still-critical take:

Mathuina, Donal P., and Johan von Schreeb. 2015. "2015 Ethical Dilemmas with Amputations after Earthquakes." UNISDR Scientific and Technical Advisory Group Case Studies. https://www.preventionweb.net/files/workspace/7935_omathunaamputation.pdf.

A comprehensive recent review of relevant empirical findings, about these events, can be found in:

Arnaouti, Matthew Keith Charalambos, Gabrielle Cahill, Michael David Baird, Laëlle Mangurat, Rachel Harris, Louidort Pierre Philippe Edme, Michelle Nyah Joseph, Tamara Worlton, Sylvio Augustin, and The Haiti Disaster Response—Junior Research Collaborative (HDR-JRC). 2022. "Medical Disaster Response: A Critical Analysis of the 2010 Haiti Earthquake." *Frontiers in Public Health.* https://www.frontiersin.org/articles/10.3389/fpubh.2022.995595.

On outcomes of prosthesis users in particular, see:

Delauche, Marie Christine, Nikki Blackwell, Hervé Le Perff, Nezha Khallaf, Joël Müller, Stéphane Callens, and Thierry Allafort Duverger. 2013. "A Prospective Study of the Outcome of Patients with Limb Trauma Following the Haitian Earthquake in 2010 at One- and Two- Year (The SuTra2 Study)." *PLoS Currents* 5 (July). https://doi.org/10.1371/currents. dis.931c4ba8e64a95907f16173603abb52f.

For some interesting ethical reflections on general issues around consent for amputation and limb salvage, see:

Humbyrd, Casey Jo, and Travis N Rieder. 2018. "Ethics and Limb Salvage: Presenting Amputation as a Treatment Option in Lower Extremity Trauma." *Journal of Bone and Joint Surgery* 100 (19): e128. https://doi.org/10.2106/jbjs.17.01522.

For a wide-ranging discussion of the ethics of international NGOs generally, see:

Rubenstein, Jennifer. 2015. *Between Samaritans and States: The Political Ethics of Humanitarian INGOs.* Oxford: Oxford University Press. https://doi.org/10.1093/acprof:oso/9780199684106.001.0001.

HOW TO KEEP HELPING, I
Taking Sides in the Arab Spring?

THE CASE

Doctors often practice in difficult conditions. Sometimes the challenges come from their own government, or the law. Physicians with *Médicins Sans Frontières* have faced these issues sharply, as have national doctors they work with, in practicing in countries experiencing civil unrest during the Arab Spring. To highlight some of the more wrenching dilemmas, consider the following, lightly fictionalized, case:

Ali, a 20-year-old male, comes to the hospital with a bleeding wound from head trauma. He is reticent to describe the cause, but there have recently been large protests in the city, and his injuries are consistent with a blow from a policeman's nightstick. ER physicians, including MSF doctors, begin treatment, but in the process the police arrive at the door, asking about patients with recent head injuries, with the clear intention of arresting dissidents.

This kind of situation can have high stakes for physicians. In Bahrain, in 2011, 13 Bahraini physicians at the al Salmaniya Medical Center were given long sentences, 15 years or more, after treating protesters during civil unrest there (Arie 2011). The government claimed that the physicians were not merely treating patients but allowing the hospital to be used as a coordinating point for protest actions.

DOI: 10.4324/9781032640525-60

INDEX